Feedback From
The Factory Floor

How managers can foster business success
An ordinary worker's opinion

By

Harley Ruft

Retired Factory Worker

Table of Contents

- Unions
- Smoking

3. The Secret to a Quality Work Life
   - Good products
   - Good marketing
   - Mutual trust
   - Mutual consideration
   - Competency

4. Summary

Preface

This book is most ordinary factory workers' fantasy. It is the ordinary worker's commentary on the dumb, nonsensical, immoral, unethical, and sometimes illegal actions of the managers who control our work life. Where do they get these people? What possesses them to do the bizarre things that they do? How is it that they have no common sense? Why did they market such a dumb product? Why can't they see that their decisions run counter to what all of us would do? How could they go with such a lame commercial? Bosses seem to select a path that is opposite to the well being of their employees and the business. However, we cannot say anything to them without risk to our livelihood and careers.

When you bid farewell to the factory floor and retire into oblivion, you can say what you think without retribution and hope that what you say changes their (managers') behavior for the better. This book is the last gasp of an ordinary worker after spending forty-three years in the thick of the action in four different US manufacturing companies.

I started on the assembly line and ended as an engineer and, throughout my career, I worked with the ordinary factory workers, mostly on manufacturing problems. I never worked as a manager, so I have never been in a position to call the shots on any part of the businesses where I worked. This is my chance. This book covers most aspects of a large U.S. manufacturing operation, presenting my opinions on what did not sit well with us factory-floor workers and how things could be done better to improve business success and the quality of work life.

This book is intended for all managers and anyone who someday dreams of being a manager. All examples come from my experiences in manufacturing factories, but I suspect that the managerial actions that we will discuss occur in most businesses. Factory workers may also want to read this book. They may feel better knowing that somebody is finally speaking out and airing the tribulations, which they silently endure. The book covers most aspects of business and personnel matters. We discuss worker and leadership competency, what goes on in human relations departments, marketing, accounting and purchasing practices, communications, company culture, product differentiation, research, engineering, and finally, quality of work life.

The purpose of this book is to show how the well-intended actions of corporate managers often miss the mark. They can make the workplace hell for us ordinary workers and they never realize it because upward communication in US industry is usually career suicide. I will present "rules" which are my opinions on how managers should respond to various business decisions. The objective of this book is a change in the way corporate America works. I want ethics to prevail in all matters; I want integrity and honesty to be contagious; I want business leaders to focus on the business; I want an end to the business chaos promulgated by hired consultants; I want equal opportunity for white males.

The foundation of this book is a set of fourteen exit essays that I wrote (at home) during the last three months of my working life. When I finally made the decision to retire, I also decided to tell the bosses at this company what I did not like about their operations, and I presented suggestions for improvement. Each essay was addressed to a vice-president and copies given to the president and CEO. I received only two written replies to my essays. One acknowledged my suggestions as something he would consider; the other showed fuming anger and told me to mind my business.

I sanitized the essays to disguise my last employer's name and business and I tried to make it impossible to identify any of the companies that I worked for. I think that my comments from the factory floor could be coming from any of the Fortune 500 or even any of the 10,000 plus US companies that are big enough to have functional departments.

I really tried to hide my anger over the things that really bothered me, and if I failed, I am sorry. However, what you are reading are the thoughts of an ordinary factory worker spilling his guts about what goes on in major corporations and similar organizations. Every word is intended to improve future business success and make work life better for employees; nothing else.

Harley Ruft

Chapter 1: The Problem with American Industry

What Happened In My Work Life?

This book chronicles the perceived changes that have occurred in the last forty-four years within the manufacturing sector of the United States' economy. Why focus on the last forty-four years? This is one person's perception, mine, and this is how long I spent in manufacturing before retiring (actually, I was urged out by an incentive). I have spent all of my adult life on the floor of factories. I started out at eighteen years old working in a small company of maybe fifty employees that made optical projectors, the kind that are still used in many classrooms. I was hired to assemble these projectors from parts that were "outsourced" in many places. The company only made the projector lens. In today's jargon, that was their "core" technology. I was not with the company long enough to know how it started, but the business seemed to be run like any typical small business in the U.S.

To build a business, a person has an idea or product. He or she starts making a product and tries to sell it. This company had projection lenses as the "product." They made lenses for movie projectors and the like, but that market was not very big, so the owner hired a consulting engineering company to design a product that used his lens. This new product line was to increase the market for the large glass lenses that the owner knew how to grind and polish. The consultant designed an opaque and a transparency projector that used the lens that was the company's core technology. The projectors had maybe one hundred parts in each. The consultant designed these, and the owner got competitive bids on all the parts. I and four other young people assembled the parts into finished projectors and packaged them for shipping. This is the type of business model now proposed by some business consultants--make very little or nothing yourself. The owner laid me off after a short time because the owner's nephew came home from college and needed a job. That is the way it works in "wholly owned" companies. Nepotism reigns. The company went out of business about ten years after my stint. I do not know why because it had the best product. We used to project the same image on the competitive projectors and this company's projector always had the best image (brightest and cleanest). I lost track because I was away at school, but these types of projectors are still being made, and a big corporation now owns most of the market in the U.S. He may have been bullied out of business. The projectors that are out there now contain fewer parts and use less-expensive optical elements. Maybe the company that I worked for lost the game because the owner did not own the technology. He bought it. He did not have the technical staff to continually improve the technology--to have the lowest cost projector that will do the job.

My first permanent factory job was with a division of one of the "big three" automobile manufacturers. In the fifties, there were more than three in the U.S. In fact, in 1957 when I started in the auto factory, there were at least eight auto manufacturers and twenty-two automobile brands. The ones that I remember are:

GM:	Chevrolet, Buick, Oldsmobile, Pontiac, Cadillac
Ford:	Mercury, Lincoln, Ford, Henry J, Edsel
Chrysler:	Dodge, Plymouth, DeSoto, Chrysler
American Motors:	Nash, Rambler, Metropolitan,

Kaiser: Frazer, Kaiser
Studebaker
Packard
Jeep

At the time of writing this book, there were nine surviving brands of cars and only two U.S. car manufacturers had survived as a separate corporation; this is one symptom of "the problem."

My five-year stint in the automotive industry was absolutely wonderful. Getting in was not easy. I applied for the cooperative engineering program that the company ran. If appointed, the job paid enough to cover tuition and expenses and ensured an engineering job at the end of the five-year program (if it was completed). Acceptance in the program hinged on high school achievement and on the results of a competitive eight-hour exam. My brother was appointed the year before me. He was assigned to an electrical components plant, and when I was appointed, I was assigned to an engine parts factory. We worked for two months, then went to school for two months at the "company college" in Michigan. We worked in different departments during each work block, and we were required to write a report on a significant project in each department. The report was graded by the department, the training director, and the school as part of the curriculum.

After my four years of school and work assignments, I had worked in every department in the plant. My fifth year consisted of working full-time on a thesis project. These projects were usually the plant's biggest technical problems. Mine was a real challenge – to reduce the scrap rate on aluminum engine castings from the then current 40% to less than 5%. I did it, but not without collaboration with the corporation's top scientists at their Detroit Technical Center.

Working in the automotive industry was exciting and fulfilling. Models changed each year and the whole plant worked as a team to get the next model out. It was very dynamic. The people were great workers, and everybody carried their share of the load. (Nobody "goofed off" because it was not tolerated.) As an example, the first time that I was assigned to work on an assembly line, I was told to take on a specific operation on the assembly line. There were about forty people on the line. They showed me how to perform my function and then started up the line. I could not miss doing my task on the engine part or it would be scrap. After two hours or so, the set-up man came to me and said, "Take a break, sonny." I walked over to a candy machine, bought a candy bar, and stood there eating it. A boss that I did not know came up to me, asked my name and where I worked, and told me to get back to my job. This is how I learned that "take a break" means hurry to the bathroom and hurry back. Nobody stood around and that was the way it was. Nobody dawdled on the computer; nobody chatted at the water cooler. People were paid well, but they earned it. They did seventy minutes of work for each hour's pay.

So what happened to this company? It still exists, but making fewer parts themselves. They now make engine systems that require only a fraction of the parts that previous engines needed. The last time that I toured the plant where I had worked, it was barren. The area that used to be alive with two thousand assembly workers was mostly warehouse with a few machines and assembly niches. The cavernous plant housed a few hundred people lucky enough to still be part of manufacturing in the U.S.

My brother's co-op plant did not fare so well. It was even busier than the engine parts factory. (In the old days, this plant was "spun off" as they say in business jargon.) It was deemed not to be "core" to the making of an automobile. They made the motors and actuators for windshield wipers, and most know these are not "core" to an automobile. This plant and other electric motor and radio plants in the corporation were sold to a non-U.S. company. The motor company had been a moneymaking plant for fifty years, but now they are losing money and are on the verge of bankruptcy although they are still the principle supplier to some of the largest auto manufacturers in the world. So part of the problem is financial shenanigans. Viable companies are traded like stock to test economists' untried business models.

When I started at what would be my last job, it was during the halcyon days of manufacturing in the U.S. I was recruited at graduate school, and I did not have to search for a job. In the spring of that year, countless companies had set up tables in the student union and to go on an expense-paid trip, one simply talked to the people in the union who were giving interview trips for engineering jobs. This is how I got my job. In fact, I ended up having to choose between three great-sounding jobs. Two offers were in my hometown; one was in a large U.S. city about three hundred miles from home. The job I chose was as a metallurgical engineer in a metallurgical laboratory in a huge manufacturing complex. There were many buildings, many different types of manufacturing: hardware, chemicals, pharmaceuticals, even a rolling mill and a huge power plant to keep the wheels turning. The plant was like a self-contained city. There was a bank, a recreation center, many sports fields, a movie theater (all the perks). The manufacturing philosophy was to make everything needed for a product on site. The shop that made piping and reactor vessels even had several blacksmiths with a forge, etc. to make special lifting hooks and similar heavy steel components.

The technical staff, of which I was a part, was top-notch. They hired only the top of the class and enforced continuing education. All engineers were encouraged to get state licenses. The research staff could work on whatever they wanted to (in a gorgeous high-rise building with a million-dollar view). Each building and manufacturing staff had their own engineers (and administration), and the plant had a huge central technical staff to engineer and build manufacturing machines, and to construct the buildings and facilities needed to house these machines. This central technical group numbered several thousand. It was a bustling place, and we were always rushing to get out new products. It was a busy, challenging, wonderful place to work.

In this type of atmosphere, people felt that they were a part of a conquering army. We strived to be better than the competition in all matters. People worked together. People knew each other and each other's families, and the company encouraged camaraderie by sponsoring countless clubs, sports teams and community events. We were all proud to work for the company, and the company was a pillar of the communities where its plants were located.

This situation prevailed for the first fifteen years of my career, through the nineteen seventies. Then an economic downturn brought the first changes in how the business was run. Management started to cut back on the company-sponsored perks. The first of these to go was the shoeshine stations from the men's room. All of the twenty or so men's rooms in the eight-story building that I worked in had a wooden shoeshine station consisting of cans of black and brown shoe polish, brushes, and a place to put your feet to polish your shoes. These stations were made from clear birch in the plant's pattern shop (yes, we used to make our own patterns for castings). I suspect that the cost of the polish and brushes was insignificant, but they were an unnecessary benefit, and because the company started to feel the need to reduce costs, they felt company-subsidized shoeshines were an excess.

Needless to say, they did not stop at shoeshine stations. The foreman's club, the superintendents' lunch, the baseball stadium, the rifle range, the bowling alleys, the noontime movies, the softball for kids, the free parking all disappeared over the next ten years or so. Employee reduction was coincident with perk reduction. Employment reductions started in about 1984 in the form of retirement incentives. They happened in a two or three year cycle until I left in 2002. The workforce by then had been reduced by about 35% of the 1980 level.

Besides the perks and employees, the company also shed businesses. The biggest was a spin-off of the company's crown jewel – a division that had been a world leader in its field for more than sixty years. This division had technology that the corporation needed to continue to manufacture their core products. In spite of the fact that my plant needed feedstock from the unit that was being spun off, they made the cut anyway. I think that what appeared to all of us as a foolhardy business decision, may have been necessary to pay the bills. When it became a separate company, it took with it several billion dollars in debt from the mother corporation. The debt came from the corporation buying businesses that they knew nothing about. Diversification was the prevailing "model" in the eighties, and car companies were buying toilet tissue companies; pharmaceuticals were buying paint companies;

chemical companies were buying insurance companies; and electrical manufacturers were buying radio stations. Five years later they were all looking to sell these adventures and to refocus on their core business.

Following this trend, the 1990's were an era of mergers. Every huge corporation was looking for a similarly huge corporation to merge with and to form a goliath corporation. The company that I worked for had not merged by the time of my retirement, but it was definitely in a downward spiral in revenues, stock price, and new products. The retirement incentives had decimated the technical staff and they had trouble making the products that they had been making for fifty years.

As a diversion (I suspect), all managers began to focus on safety meetings and diversity. Employees could get fired if they got hurt running a machine, so we had to carry first aid supplies and doctor ourselves when we got cut or got a sliver. The diversity movement replaced most managers with people who had a preferred (by managers) gender or ethnicity. Many were hired from outside, unrelated companies.

In my thirty-eight year career, the company went from respected world leader in their field with loyal-til-death employees, to a stumbling, declining corporation that seems to be having trouble making anything. The non-diversity employees would rather work someplace else. The company's newest manufacturing complex, five million square feet on four hundred acres, stands empty like a vacated city. It is a huge complex and a wonderful work environment, but it was too costly to keep. It was not spun off, but emptied of people and machines and sold to a real estate developer. The stock price, which ranged from one hundred to one hundred fifty dollars per share when I started, fell to twenty to thirty dollars per share when I left.

These tales of woe concerning American industry can be repeated by millions of Americans in hundreds of cities. The details of the demise of these manufacturing companies vary with the locale, still there are literally millions of American factory workers like me who witnessed the fall of great companies and were helpless to stop it.

This is the problem. America became a successful nation and a great place to live because of its manufacturing base. Manufacturing industries created jobs that people could dedicate their lives to and, which rewarded them with remuneration that allowed them enough money to marry, to buy homes, to raise children, and to build communities. America cannot continue to exist at its current standard of living on XX-Mart jobs. It cannot happen. Yet, we seem to be going in that direction; which is a shame.

Why this book?

I have been a silent anonymous observer of what goes on in typical large manufacturing organizations, and I gradually developed the intense belief that most business failures in manufacturing are self-inflicted. Managers become clueless; they do not know the business; they do not know what goes on at the factory floor level; they do not know how to select talent; they do not know what to spend their time on; they do not have the skills for the job they are in; and finally, they do not use what my wife calls "common sense." I have been observing these things for more than forty years. I have never been part of management so I have always been on the receiving end of mandates, business plans, restructures and the like. I think that it may be helpful to honest managers if they knew what employees think about their management decisions. We never tell them how we feel while it would be risking the loss of a raise or our jobs to disagree with what they plan. In general, when we factory-floor workers leave the company, we move on to other pursuits and never give our previous employer honest feedback. This book, however, is honest feedback from the factory floor to management regarding decisions in manufacturing industries. We see that plans are not working out, but nobody tells. We see dishonest managers, but nobody tells. We see injustice in employee treatment, but nobody tells. We witness incredible waste, but nobody tells! We see decisions that violate common sense – and nobody tells. I am telling. I do not plan to work in manufacturing again. I plan to live out whatever time is left on my pension and Social Security. I am in a position to criticize the CEO of my former employing company because I do not need his weekly paycheck. I am in a position to tell him how to run the corporation because I know what works and does not work at the factory floor level. And, as anybody in manufacturing should know, if you do not have your workers with you, they will be against you, and you will fail.

The plan

I have been collecting snippets for this book for more than twenty years. I have kept a file ever since my last employer started to do "dumb stuff." I vowed that some day I would write a book about corporate "mistakes" because they keep proliferating them. I assume that they do not realize that things like shutting down the employee suggestion system are just plain stupid, which nobody has the guts to tell them. I will tell "them," the managers of American manufacturing companies, what makes no sense to us workers on the factory floor. I cannot divulge the names of the corporations that I worked for in my career for legal reasons, so in this book, I will refer to my last employer as "my company."

When I retired, I had to sign a document that I cannot understand because it is written in legal jargon. I was told that it said that I could not sue the corporation for anything that they did to me, that I will never say anything bad about the company and, of course, that I will never do anything to aid a competitor of the company or compete with it myself. A violation would mean that I have to return the year's severance pay that they gave me. This was the standard "good bye" for a lifetime of service and loyalty.

My company was an old multinational corporation with annual sales in excess of a billion dollars and more than ten thousand employees. I am addressing this book to companies of all sizes, although the larger ones are most susceptible to adoption of practices that I believe destroy a business. Unfortunately, here in the United States, the management faults cited in this book apply even more than in industry. I have been involved with the government of the town where I live for more than 35 years and I have learned that much of what democratic governments do is in violation of ethics and common sense. Therefore our unsolicited advice from the factory floor also applies to most large organizations.

I was given only two weeks to decide if I should take my company's retirement incentive, but I could stay on for sixty days after signing the papers, to clean up. I decided to retire, due mostly to the fact that because I worked almost exclusively on development projects. My funds for these projects had been reduced to zero, and there were no identified sources of funding on the horizon. I was funded out of the corporation. Anyway, in my remaining sixty days I wrote a series of exit essays to the vice-presidents. Essentially, I summarized what I thought was wrong with a particular function, like marketing, and suggested improvements, and I sent copies to the CEO and president. I received only two replies, so most of the essays were probably discarded as rantings from a disgruntled retiree. I tried to limit these essays to no more than two pages so that they might get read. Now that I have a full yellow pad to devote to each subject, I will explain a bit more why I think they needed changes in these areas and suggest even more improvements. The format of this book will be to start most chapters with my exit essay, edited to remove names and places, and then to develop the topic of the exit essay in more detail. The exit essays covered these subjects: company leadership, new products, technical competency, marketing, purchasing, accounting, company culture, programs, human resources, employee communications, diversity, research, engineering, and work-life quality. In addition, I will present some views on unions, cubicles, dealing with foreign competition, computers, ethics, and industrial psychology. I hope that I do not create another "bad business model" like the ones that got U.S. manufacturing in trouble. My intent is to save U.S. industry.

Chapter 2: Leadership Competency

Rationale:

The format of this book is to present an exit essay from my last hours in corporate America and then to expand on the essay subject. We will try to convince all corporate leaders who read this book that there are better ways to run a company. Chapter subjects came from a list that I compiled on the cover of a loose-leaf binder over a period of six weeks or so. I asked, "What's wrong with this company?" I ended up with quite a long list, maybe thirty topics. I then reduced, combined, and prioritized them. Then I spilled my guts to company management in fourteen exit essays. Each essay ends with suggestions on how to do things better. It may sound as though I am of the opinion that the company that I worked for did everything wrong. Of course they did some things right, but not enough.

How is it that I know how to run a corporation and the people who run them do not? I guess it is a gift. Of course, this is a facetious answer, but the real situation is that most of the management decisions that I was subjected to over the past fifteen years seemed to defy common sense and to be contrary to the way that my co-workers and I thought things should be done. We should be right since the company was certainly not doing well by the measures of corporate success that we factory workers understood (cash on hand, debt, sales, profits, stock price, and dividends). All of these things had been declining for many years. For example, in the early sixties, after I started with my last employer, my wife and I put all our savings into company stock. We figured it would grow enough to pay for college for our three sons. We let our investment ride for thirty-five years. Dividends were invested in more stock. It did not pay for our sons' colleges. We sold all of our company stock in 2000 and we did not end up with a significant profit, only about two times our original investment. If we had put the money in an ordinary savings account, we would easily have increased our original investment by a factor of ten. Why would anybody buy stock in this company?

RULE: Never hold onto stock like it was a piece of heirloom furniture. Consider the stock market as legalized gambling, and only gamble what you can afford to lose.

Another aspect of this book is to present "rules" that are essentially my personal opinion on a subject presented. They reflect my life experience. The only worth of age is "possible" wisdom. I can tell younger people not to gamble money that they need in the stock market because I saw what happened in my case, and I also recently witnessed acquaintances losing their retirement savings because they invested all in their company's stock, and the company went bankrupt, making their stock investment worthless. Now the financial advisors are preaching to put no more than 5% of your "gambling dollars" in any one investment.

So, the rule and this discussion are like a sidebar in a textbook. They are nuggets of wisdom learned the hard way, and I would like to pass them along. They may not always occur in the right place or time in this book, however, I inserted them where I did so I wouldn't forget them. Mostly, I will try to make these rules apply to the subject at hand. If they do not, forgive me. I am retired and retired people can do these kinds of things because the strife is over. We do not have to do things that lead to personal success. Our success in our chosen line of work has been determined by what we did in our forty-five years of regular work life. These were the years that determined our possessions and social status.

Exit Essay On Unqualified Leadership

Now, returning to what started to be the subject of this chapter – leadership competency. Essentially, this relates to whether or not managers have the tools to do their jobs. If you are going to work as a chef, you should know how to cook. If you are going to be a secretary, you should know how to type and use PC software. If you are going to be an engineer, you should successfully complete an accredited engineering curriculum. This may seem obvious, but apparently, many managers in American industry do not think so. Here is my exit essay on the subject.

Exit Essay: **The Root Cause of the Company's Current Business Problems: Unqualified Leadership – A View from the Factory Floor**

I define an unqualified leader as a person who has been placed in charge of others because of a favorable relationship with a superior or because of a particular birth circumstance or proclivity. Job skills, job knowledge, related experience, related education, related training, intelligence and interpersonal skills were not the deciding factor in the selection process. In simpler terms, the biggest suck-up in the department was made boss or a person was made a boss because he or she fulfilled a superior's perception of desirable ethnicity, gender, age, sexual preference or other "non-talent."

The practice of giving leadership positions to suck-ups has, by my observation, been part of the company's culture for the past two decades. Manager positions are usually not posted. *A manager who is moving on recommends a person to take his or her position and it matters not if the department employees feel that they can trust and support the assigned manager. Leader selection has been a "backroom" decision. Also, once a manager has been created, he or she usually has the title for life. If a department goes away, the manager is given another department. It matters not what the department does, or if the manager has any skills that apply.*

Creating managers because of a birth circumstance or other "non talents" is a more recent part of the company culture. Though well intentioned, this practice is unethical, illegal in the USA, and an absolute violation of fairness to all employees and stockholders. The employees who were passed over because they did not have the right gender, race, etc. never forget this, and the company ends up with an organization that is a great place to work if you are one of the chosen diversities, and an intolerable place to work for the rest. The deselected have no hope of joining the company's leadership ranks. Selective diversity is discrimination and a company that practices discrimination will fail.

When I started at the company in the nineteen sixties, a person earned a management position by excelling in his or her department, field of expertise, or he or she excelled in another company. A manager may have been the best scientist, the best engineer, the best financial person, the best people person, or the most-trusted coworker as assessed by peers. Early in my career, I was occasionally asked to attend management meetings on a particular problem. The meetings were held in the walnut-paneled rooms on the second floor of the "ivory tower." I used to sit in awe at the breath of knowledge that the managers had. They seemed to know every aspect of the business.

Now we have managers who often do not even know what is made in departments that they manage.

I have had five supervisors in the past fifteen years (in the same department) and four out of the five were unqualified leaders in my opinion. For the past twenty years or so, here on the factory floor, the company has been promoting the least of our numbers – often charlatans, to manager positions, and the company is seeing the results of this practice. They cannot run the company.

What is the solution? Do not discriminate. Seek out the company's best as leaders. Post leadership positions as they arise on company job listings. Let everyone apply; open the company to all employees. Establish a search committee for each leadership position. This search committee should include some employees of the department that is seeking a leader. The search committee, using criteria that the committee establishes, should screen candidates. Final leader selection should reflect the consensus of the search committee. Many USA universities use this system for selecting department heads, and unquestionably the United States has the finest higher education system in the world.

The company's survival hinges on what happens in the next year or two in its leadership ranks. The company's best people, not charlatans, not politically correct people, must be sought out and put in leadership positions. The company must stop discrimination against older workers and people who through no fault of their own are not among selected minorities. The company needs its best performers calling the plays. If not, we will lose. This is my opinion.

Main Reasons for Incompetence

This essay was e-mailed to a vice-president with copies to the CEO and president. I did not hear from any of the addressees, probably because the tone was rather angry. The main problem that I was trying to address is giving leadership to people who lack the competency and skills needed to lead others. Most promotions were given to suck-ups and to people who had what I call a favorable birth circumstance or persuasion. Favorable birth circumstance is a euphemism for selection based upon race, gender, or sexual persuasion. The company started a program in the late 1990's to make a significant percentage of its managers African American, Hispanic, or women. Somehow this program expanded to include people who advertise their sexual proclivities. So when a management position became available, the manager in charge of making the selection was eventually mandated to select from one of these people. I have no idea how managers determine a person's sexual proclivities; I suspect that they advertise in newspapers and other media that cater to people who advertise their sex life.

Selection based upon race is more clear-cut. Human Relations people have trained recruiters on how to identify people of the sought after races. One of my sons went through one such training session when he did some recruiting for a big company. They told him what questions to ask and how to interpret answers to determine if he had discovered a person with authentic racial desirability. The argument for having these programs is that a diverse workforce will be more successful than a workplace with a preponderance of a particular race. We will devote a whole chapter on this subject later. At this point, let me summarize by saying that this practice is not ethical. It is not honest. Corporate officers have an obligation to grow the company and produce ever-increasing profits to company owners – the shareholders. Putting people in leadership positions because of their sociological status rather than their ability to lead makes no sense. This practice is particularly damaging on the factory floor. Ordinary workers do not feel very good about never having an opportunity to be boss because they are not a designated minority. Similarly, they do not appreciate that their jobs are being jeopardized because their minority manager may not have the skills to keep the department viable. I have even heard minority managers complain that they were being set up for failure. They knew they could not do the job. There is just no ethic in this practice.

How to Recognize Suck-Ups

Nepotism is sucking-up to relatives. I lost my first factory job because the owner's nephew needed a job. He or his family had convinced the owner that he should fire the stranger (me) and give the job to family. Nepotism often leads to incompetent leadership, and like birth circumstance and sexual proclivity, is not ethical, honest or smart. Hiring relatives may seem like a good idea, but it is favoritism and favoritism never sits well on the factory floor.

Suck-ups are the worst problem in many businesses; worse than wrongly hired friends or family. The human relations term for suck-ups is "favorites." A standard question in HR surveys is: "Does your supervisor have favorites that he or she treats differently from the rest?" Of course, all but the suck-ups answer "yes." There is a fundamental problem with suck-ups that requires some in-depth thinking. Everybody in a leadership position likes to see his or her mandates followed. How do you identify those that are complying from those that are seeking special treatment? The short answer is that they only do what the manager mandates, but very little other work.

About fifteen years ago, I started studying charlatan behavior patterns. I identified patterns and a methodology. Here are some behavior patterns that I observed:

1. They always make it known that they agree with the managers in group meetings.
2. They conjure up questions to ask the manager in private.
3. They offer to do "dirty work" for the manager "Let me run the annual charity drive."
4. They become knowledgeable about the manager's family, hobbies, and interests – and he or she makes his or her hobbies the same.
5. They often move to the same community/neighborhood as inhabited be immediate or above managers.
6. They do the manager's work whenever possible.
7. They dress like their manager (sloppy, neat, conservative, etc.).
8. They drop all other activities to work on the manager's work.
9. They try to meet with the manager at least daily.
10. They wear penny loafers (men) or white sweaters (women).

Typically, these people have few skills other than those required for endearing themselves to managers. They usually have less than the education required for the job. They usually have few talents needed by the company to make profits and often spend much of their workday schmoozing. I consider them to be dishonest simply because not doing the work one was hired to do is stealing from the company. They take an hour's pay from the company and give the company an hour of idle patter in return.

I have encountered a number of master charlatans over the years, and it never ceases to amaze me that managers can be so completely taken in by their deceitful ways. I have had co-workers who spent their day surfing the net, with pauses only to drop in the manager's office for a social chat. I witnessed charlatans report to the big boss on the same project for several years after it was complete. There was always at last ten of us in the room when he would recycle his only project. We all knew that this work was done years earlier and so did our immediate manager, still he let his favorite snow the director.

We also had a "clutch maker" in our department. To illustrate the role of a "clutch maker," I'll relate a story that has been told many times about a new captain on a US navel ship. He toured the crew and asked each person what he or she did at his or her respective station. One compartment was filled with a large computer-looking machine with some reel-to-reel tape drives, lots of knobs, and a plethora of flashing lights. The captain asked: "What is your job, sailor?" "Clutch-maker First Class, Sir." "Carry on," was the captain's reply. This same thing happened when two other captains took charge of the ship. The fourth new captain was not as easy to satisfy. He asked the clutch-maker to give him a demonstration of what he did at 0800 in the morning. The captain and other officers gathered on the deck where the sailor brought his elegant machine. It was humming and its lights were flashing. Suddenly, the ship hit a large swell and heeled about five degrees to port. The elegant machine slid down the deck into the ocean and went C L U U T C H H H H. My old department still has such a clutch maker, and I have witnessed five managers come and go without asking for a demonstration of what he does.

In summary, the company will not get what it should from a department when an incompetent leader and poor morale permeate all activities. People will not give their all under such circumstances. Suck-ups are the people who meet daily with the boss, agree with him or her on all matters, do the boss' busy work, and essentially, do very little to no real work, work which the company's customers would be willing to pay for.

RULE: Identify suck-ups and find out why they need to do it.

Dealing With Suck-Ups

My exit essay suggests dealing with suck-ups by using college-type search committees to select managers. I firmly believe in promoting people to leadership positions based upon training, talent, education, personality, and ethics. Suck-ups usually are short on all of these attributes. I suggest that managers who are seeking a new manager use a ranking matrix that quantifies all of the attributes needed for a particular management position and then seek documentation to support the ranking. In the area of communications, ask for examples of reports, papers, proposals, etc. In the area of education, have candidates list completed college educational courses/degrees. In the area of expertise, have the candidate demonstrate his or her expertise. Test their ability to deal with others by interviewing the people that he or she has had working relations with. Check teamwork capability with similar interviews. Form your own opinion on demeanor by questioning leadership candidates in such a manner that would make apparent if a person is thoughtful, easily perturbed, can or cannot think fast, and in general, behave in a civil manner at all times.

The best way to deal with suck-ups, however, is to analyze them. People are products of their environment. If a person is not very smart all through his or her life, he or she may suck up to a parent, teacher or coach to compensate. The best hitter on a baseball team does not have to suck up to the coach to get into the starting lineup. A lousy hitter does. Probe people's youth and see if you can pinpoint why they might have to suck up.

Also, analyze yourself to determine why you may be susceptible to manipulation by one of these people. Can you be manipulated (excluding by your mate)? Do you have character weaknesses that they can exploit? Are you basically lazy and enjoy pawning off your busy work? Do you have an inferiority complex and need phony reinforcements from these people? Are you too weak to lead and so use these underlings to do your job? Do you not have real friends and rely on suck-ups to be faux-friends? Are you unsure in your mandates and need a suck-up to tell you what to do? If you, as a manager, can say, "yes" to some of these questions, it may be unethical and dishonest for you to continue as a manager.

> **RULE:** If you are too weak or lack the skills to lead, then don't try.
> Become an individual contributor.

Assuming that you do not have any psychological factors to cause a tendency in you to be the victim of charlatans, what positive actions can you take to prevent being possessed?

Here are some:

1. Analyze subordinates' intentions when they ask to speak to you.
2. Be observant of the "real work" that suck-ups do.
3. Excuse yourself from unannounced intrusions by suck-ups. (i.e., "I cannot talk now, please see my secretary to schedule a time.")
4. Establish an arms-length relationship with all subordinates.
5. Minimize informal patter with subordinates.
6. Lunch alone or with management peers.
7. Have regular one-on-one meetings with all subordinates.
8. Examine all actions and ask if they are fair to everyone in the department/organization.
9. Encourage opinions from all subordinates.
10. Explain your rationale on all major decisions.

These can probably be distilled into a rule.

> **RULE:** Never show favoritism.

Why Promoting Favorites Is So Destructive

I started my campaign to save my last employer when an old college classmate was hired from retirement (he was

CEO of another large company) as an executive vice-president. I thought that I might now have somebody in upper management who would listen to my warnings about how things were deteriorating on the factory floor. He told me that he read all of my e-mails and to keep writing my opinions on company directions. In doing so, one of my e-mails (to my friend) got into the hands of another VP who was not interested in my opinions. He cascaded this down the corporate ladder, and my manager's boss, the division director, called me onto the carpet. He told me that he never speaks out against directives from his superiors, [He felt] that because they were above him in the corporate ladder, they must know more than me, so I never question their decisions." He made it very clear that his subordinates (me) should never question his decisions. He expected blind obedience from everyone under him in the organization chart. He advised, "Keep your head down and your mouth shut."

I didn't take his advice, and that is why I am retired. In my opinion (which my old director does not want), a key part of any organization's success is having everyone contribute his or her ideas. I have directed countless engineering projects over forty plus years in the business, and I can honestly state that the project was always made more successful because of suggestions from whom my arrogant director considered to be subordinates who should have given me blind obedience. I designed countless test machines to be used in my laboratory studies, and I cannot remember one that did not contain a "screw up" on my part. These test machines were built by the machinist who was part of "my team," and he would always identify flaws on the design before the chips were made. He would say, "This is not going to work, this hits here, etc." These machinists made the machines work so that we both benefited, and the company benefited as well. The machinist could be proud to point to a well running machine that he made and say, "I built that." I could say, "I designed it," even though my original design did not work. The company gained when we used the machine to solve a production problem. It was a win-win situation all around. The same type of thing happened with the technicians who did the actual testing on my projects. The technicians who were team players would always give me daily feedback on experiments. He or she would tell me immediately when an experiment that I designed was not working. We would get together, find the problem, and develop a new plan. Similarly, there was almost never an experiment that worked as originally planned, and we ended up using project plans with significant technician input.

However, not all of my projects had a support staff that contributed. I have had technicians do long experiments following my instructions to the letter and ended up with no results and a failed project. I will never forget one that took three months and scores of tests. Every time I would ask the technician how the experiment was going, she would say, "Everything is going great. I have the data on material A, B & C. I'll start D tomorrow." Any problems? No. Well, when materials A through C were all tested, she tabulated the data for my analysis. There was so much variability in the test data that all of it was worthless. The test was not working, and she never told me. I looked like a jerk, she lost my respect as a technician, and the company wasted a lot of money. The technician was giving me blind obedience.

Another cost of unqualified leaders is working on the wrong things, things that your customer would not pay for. One boss that I had was completely clueless about department business. Consequently, all department meetings and projects were aimed at safety, department layout, cleanups, scheduling meetings, and other fluff. There was no mention of the business. Technical problems, needed technologies, workloads, equipment issues, and technical training were never discussed. The most important project in the department was placement of safety glass containers for guests. This unqualified leader had us all focusing on burden activities rather than on activities that had to do with making money for the company.

I witnessed this same sort of thing at the division level. A person was brought out of nowhere to take over complete operation of a division with almost 15,000 employees. We had no idea where this woman came from, and we suspected that she got the job even though she was not qualified. She focused on improving the plant grounds. She had little parks created, tore down good buildings, and spent a fortune on landscaping. All this was being done while we workers were not allowed to spend a penny on capital equipment or even needed maintenance on existing equipment. She was eventually fired, but only after she went 100 million dollars over budget on a moving operation. She was not qualified for the job she was given and both parties lost. She lost her reputation, and the company lost a lot of money. In addition, many of us ordinary workers were not too happy about the fact that advancement is not based upon qualifications.

Certainly, competent leaders usually earn their positions. They are open and encourage suggestions from subordinates. They strive to know the business and they do not reinforce suck-ups. They seek to surround themselves with people who are smarter. They talk to workers at all levels as equals. They try to know something about each subordinate as an individual. They strive to identify talent and use that talent in the best interest of the company.

They present their work ethic and moral behavior as a model for their subordinates. Above all, to be competent, a leader must know the business that he or she is leading. This is fundamental. If you are to be the leader of an engineering department, you must have an engineering degree and significant experience in the field. If you are going to lead a machine shop, you must have run machines and worked in the business. This opinion runs counter to current human relations thinking in most US industry. I suspect that they promote the concept that a leader can lead anything because most managers have no training or education in their field.

Perhaps the reason I feel so strongly about knowing what you lead is because of my neighbor. He was an economist with a great personality and presence. He worked his way up to the presidency of a large 75-year-old clothing manufacturing company even though he knew nothing at all about cloth and tailoring. It went out of business within a few years. He moved on to the presidency of a 100-year-old leather goods manufacturing company with the same results. He then became the CEO of a 50-year-old printing company. Again, the same thing happened. He then moved on to a job in a company that made chemical filters. I lost track of him after that because he moved, but I suspect that this company fared similarly.

> **RULE:** Know the business that you want to lead.

Chapter 3: Product Differentiation

As part of my "save the company" program, I have
attended many classes and courses on business practices,
management techniques, and industrial psychology.
However, a single two-hour lecture by a successful retired
local entrepreneur thoroughly convinced me that product
differentiation is a mandatory part of business success in
the manufacturing sector. In the service sector, it is service
differentiation and in government, it is elected candidate
differentiation. My definition of product differentiation is
that a company makes a product that has desirable and
needed features not found in the competitor's product. This
does not mean more features. Many times too many
features make the product a failure. For example, I once
bought some data recorders that had a button that could be
pressed in different ways to program the instrument to
come on at different times, record data, shut itself off, send
the data to a PC and on and on and on. The manipulation
of this single button was beyond all of our best technicians
and after trying to use these devices that cost $2,000.00 for
several months, the technicians put them into the cabinet in
the back of the lab that was relegated to equipment that did
not work. This is not an isolated case. I am writing this in
an airport waiting for a plane. Just this morning, I
encountered a new shower control in a brand new hotel that
is an example of a product that I deemed to be deficient
because it had new features known only to the designer.
You guessed it. It took me fifteen minutes to figure out
how to turn it on. When it was turned on, it took another
fifteen minutes to figure out how to move the single control
handle to prevent scalding or freezing; certainly an
inappropriate product for a hotel near an airport with a
customer base that includes visitors from San Jose and
Afghanistan.

> **RULE:** More features does not insure
> differentiation.

Each of you undoubtedly could insert your own case history of a product made bad by too many or unwanted features. I am not sure that my corollary to the above rule would be accepted by all business schools, but what the hell, here it is:

> **RULE:** If it requires instructions, a manual, or
> assembly, it will not be a "winner"
> product.

Of course, some products like a Boeing 727 need some user training, but if I must read something to make a product work; I usually do not buy it. Simplicity usually produces favorable differentiation.

Now that I have vented my displeasure from this morning's hotel incident, let us get back to the subject at hand: the definition of product differentiation. The lecture on differentiation that I referred to at the start was given by an engineer who worked for a big company. He got frustrated by the largeness and lack of new products in his company and took the bold move of starting his own company. He went into detail about the usual money and family problems, but spent most of his time hammering home how he made his product (an electronic device) better than the competition. He did not talk about it, but I left the class with the belief that market sector is part of differentiation. His company became successful and too large for him to handle as an owner, so it is now a major corporation. He is wealthy, but no longer involved. As far as I can see, this company is still successful because it makes a product that no one else makes. Their electronic devices are mostly used by the military so the customer base is the 500 or so countries that we have on our planet. To me, this is a niche market. I know of a nearby company, which has been in business for almost a hundred years making a profit, using the same building, and manufacturing equipment installed in 1906. They are the only manufacturer in the world of a sheet metal toy that is only sold at Christmas time. Christmas sales have been supporting the owner's family and their few trusted employees for a long time. They have product differentiation by exclusion. Nobody else wants to bother to make this product.

In summary, product differentiation means that a company produces a product that is simple, offers needed benefits over the competition, or serves an exclusive market sector. So what's the problem? The problem that prompted this chapter was that my company (note: I am only using "my" to save writing "the company that I retired from." It really is not my company) lost their product differentiation in most product lines. They used to have product differentiation in quality. They had only a handful of worldwide competitors, but they could not keep their "better quality" differentiation because their quality simply degraded. It degraded because of some of the problems addressed in other chapters, but degradation of quality has become epidemic in many companies, services, and government organization so what we have to say on this subject has wide application.

The problem that we are trying to address is loss of jobs, lack of new products, and lack of progress in making life easier and better. At the time of writing this chapter, the largest accounting company in the US was disintegrating (with 118,000 employees). It was falling apart because of alleged impropriety at a very high management level. This company's product differentiation was integrity. A US government indictment against the company degraded its integrity. An hour after I returned my rental car this morning, I read in the newspaper that the company had just filed for bankruptcy. It used to be the low-cost rental agency. I noticed over the past few years that their prices were increasing significantly. Apparently, so have others. They lost their differentiation – lower cost.

What will we say to make managers refocus on product differentiation? We will start with my exit essay to my company and follow with other cosmic truths that I think of after rereading my exit essay.

Exit Essay: *New Products and Product Differentiation – A View from the Factory Floor*

In my early years in the company, I remember that we used to be very busy in the fall with making sure that we had adequate manufacturing facilities for the new products that would be showcased for the Christmas buying season. The number and frequency of new consumer products has been steadily declining to the point where there are no really new products, and the old products have no features to differentiate them from the competition. Most of the products we make are also made by somebody else, and our products are usually identical to the competition. Only the packaging has anything to do with the company. Our consumer product quality has slipped so far that there is negative differentiation in many cases; we are lower quality than the competition. At our recent engineering conference, I heard our chief marketing officer state that the company is no longer a consumer-product company. We are a service company specializing in "Datamation."* I am not a businessperson, but I wager that I can ask one hundred people on the street if they know what

"Datamation" means and none will know. Our marketing chief also showed some of the company's new commercials. My reaction was: What are we selling? I have no idea. He said that these commercials were aimed at businesses, not consumers. Well, I own two small businesses, and I still do not know what it is trying to sell me. I guess that I will not buy whatever it is that the company is selling.

What should the company do about product differentiation?

What should the company do about consumer products?

What should the company do about selling services?

I have one answer for all three questions: Establish a real product-engineering function. The responsibility for new products and services is scattered in hundreds of cubicles in dozens of buildings and in a score of worldwide sites. All operate independently of each other. Each business unit does its own thing. A product engineer in one organization may be a line operator who made a particular product for a number of years. There is no real product engineering in many business units, only product maintenance. New products often come from the purchasing department. They buy the new products that carry the "made in China" imprint under the company logo. The company is not developing new products in the business that grew the company, and the services that we claim to sell are certainly questionable as a source of revenue. I have heard nothing but complaints from users of our software and services. Our own facilities in our core businesses are an embarrassment.

What do I mean by a product engineering function? Product engineering in my definition is a corporate function staffed with graduate engineers and scientists and

*their only job is to continually improve existing products
and to develop new products to grow a particular business
or start a new business. The product engineers know the
science of their products; they know the customers; they
know the manufacturing processes available; they know the
market; they are capable designers, and above all they are
innovative people. Not everybody can be a product
engineer. It takes people who have a history of creativity.*

*The company probably has some people that could be good
product engineers, but they are cocooned in the business
units. Unit A product engineers do not talk with Unit B
engineers, who do not talk with Unit C engineers, who do
not talk with Unit D engineers, who do not talk with the
systems engineers, and nobody talks with the
"Datamation" engineers whoever and wherever they are.
There is no collaboration. There are no common thrusts or
product platforms. We make similar products in five
business units using different chassis. Why not one? Our
products have different packaging systems. Why not one?
The company's software products hardly make it to market
before they are canceled. We seem to have product chaos
in this area. We are our own worst enemy because we do
not collaborate and share inventive talent.*

*What is the solution? I suggest a Product Engineering
Department staffed by product engineers that exist in the
existing business unit silos. They can stay where they are,
but they will report to the management of the product
engineering function. The manager of the product
engineering function has the responsibility for a continuous
stream of new products and services that work in the
marketplace and make significant profits. The manager of
product engineering should probably report to the
executive committee. The company needs to establish a
focus on new products and to fix the broken ones. The*

product engineering function would also be responsible for quality audits on what is currently being produced and for the correction of problems that can be fixed with a product change.

In summary, in my opinion the company is in a downward spiral, and one of the fundamental reasons is a dearth of fresh, new consumer products and no differentiation in existing products. These problems are compounded by an imaginary service strategy. This market only exists in the minds of the few people who made up the "Datamation" word. The company needs to establish a department that has overall responsibility for new products and the quality of existing products. We have been decentralizing into an unmanageable morass in product development. We have lost focus as a company of the purpose of the company. We are fantasizing about making money in ventures that we know nothing about, and we are ignoring the business that we used to know better than all others. The company must return to its roots to survive – my opinion.

*Not the word proposed by the company but a synonym.

Essay Reflection

Wow! I sounded pretty impassioned about a product engineering function. And I am. I am also very upset that we moved from making new products to buying them in a country where the labor costs are a fraction of the costs in the USA. I am the eternal optimist. I think that anybody can succeed if you significantly invest yourself in reaching your goal. In other words, the company did not have to "cop out" and buy their new products from companies in nations with labor rates that allow engineering and development activities. I think that the company could muster enough talent to design "winner" products if they changed the corporate structure to consolidate product-engineering talent. Subassemblies or components may be manufactured in countries with low labor rates to keep costs down, but it would be a company product, not a designed and made-in-China product with only a company package.

This may not be the best place for my comments on manufacturing in so-called "Third-World Nations," but here they are. First of all, the term "Third World" is denigrating and certainly an insult to the countries so branded. It is a stupid term. People are the same in all countries; only some have worse governments than others. I made an unforgettable trip to China in 1985. I participated in a scientific mission sponsored jointly by the National Science Foundation and the Chinese Academy of Sciences. I spent three weeks seeing the China that foreigners seldom see. The people were wonderful; the government was stern, but benevolent. People were not allowed to do what they want, but the government would not let anybody starve. They tried to provide a job for every person who wanted one. I never agreed with communism as the economic plan for a country, but by the end of my visit, I formed the opinion that Communism, at least provided the order necessary to feed over a billion people. They had crops planted absolutely everywhere, even on rooftops. The people had few possessions, but appeared to be happy (people everywhere were chattering and smiling) and there was an abundance of food in the free markets.

At the time China had two economies, by my observation. From sun-up to 8:00 in the morning, people were bustling in the streets and products were sold from street corners everywhere. Each peasant was given ten square meters of land to grow whatever they wanted and this is what was sold in the free markets (plus "products" made by people in their homes). People worked for the government in offices, institutes, factories, and communes from 8:00 to 5:00. People did not seem to care about quality in their 8:00 to 5:00 jobs because they would be paid their $60.00 per month if they knocked themselves out or not. Of course, this is an insurmountable flaw of Communism.

I have not been back to China since, but my company now has manufacturing plants in China and the wages are still only about $100.00 per month. Needless-to-say, US manufacturers cannot pay assembly line workers wages of $2000.00 per month plus significant benefit costs and compete with products assembled by Chinese getting $100.00 per month. There is no current alternative to low-cost nation assembly on products that require significant assembly labor, but the economic world leaders need to address this issue. It will not go away. Here is my unvarnished, unabridged opinion. Use of low-cost nations for manufacturing is unethical, even immoral, and should be stopped. In the United States it is almost impossible to buy a piece of clothing or electrical anything that was not made in China. The Chinese people have become the slaves of the so-called industrialized countries. They cannot strike for higher wages. They cannot own land; they cannot select leaders who will improve their living conditions; they cannot have the career path that they want. How would you like to be told to live in this hut and work at the Shinzang iron works as a riveter until we order you to another job? How would you like to be limited to one offspring? How would you like to have the state as your creator and subject of worship?

The Chinese are attempting to improve the standard of living of their people by having them become the manufacturers to the world. They will succeed if we do nothing. We will lose the technical skills needed to be manufacturers. They will have them, and they will be in a position to charge any price for manufactured items. We will become the slaves of the electronic Chinese. Preposterous? They are very smart people and I think that this is their long-term strategy. They can succeed if we do nothing.

Now back to differentiation. The main issue at my company is that they did not have an orderly methodology or defined responsibility for product development. Products seem to evolve from a swampland and who had responsibility for a particular product was a secret. We had what I term product chaos. Product chaos does not lead to differentiation. My exit essay suggested ways for my company to deal with their differentiation problem. The remainder of this chapter presents suggestions for other companies.

Differentiation By Assumption

One of the most disconcerting aspects of my company's business strategy was to assume that they could take an existing product and decide to make it and take over a significant part of the market and make money at it. They tried this with a complicated business product. They tried to differentiate by making a faster machine. After twenty years and billions of capital dollars, they conceded that they did not have enough product differentiation to make money and sold what was left of the faltering business. They did the same in a product like that was as far from the company's core business as possible, like McDonald's selling caskets. This venture resulted in about seven billion dollars in debt and a lot of restructuring and selling to get rid of the "alien business" that they bought.

What kind of arrogance does it take to think that because you are CEO, president and vice-president of a large company that you can buy a business that you do not know anything about and produce products in those businesses that are better than the competitors? I never met the big bosses who made these decisions, but I suspect that their egos overwhelmed their intelligence, business acumen and common sense. When I retired, the company was up to its ears in trying to copy products invented and made by others for a long time. Of the ventures that I was aware of, they were also using small clusters of engineers and certainly not tapping the full technical resources of the company.

> **RULE:** A company cannot produce product differentiation by assuming that they will make it better than their competition.

True product differentiation, first requires learning the business. Some take years or decades to learn. Every business has its quirks. About twenty years ago, my wife and I decided to buy rental real estate. This is the simplist business that there is (on paper). Just buy properties and rent them. Needless-to-say, we learned that this business is not as simple as it looked. We decided to differentiate by only buying small two-bedroom houses that would not be attractive to families with a herd of destructive kids. I will not go into our tales of woe in the business. We are still surviving, but certainly not because we assumed that we could do renting better than our competition. Our survival was really dumb luck. We did not have a plan to differentiate from the competition. We really only bought small two-story houses because I did not want the challenge of maintaining large houses. Further, my biggest ladder only extended to sixteen feet, not high enough to work on a three-story "dumper".

In summary, it is really risky business to try to get into a business that is significantly different from what you do most of the time. You will have to learn the vagaries of the business to survive and by then you may not have sufficient talent or resources to produce a product or service that differentiate. Be the best in what you know.

How To Achieve Product/Market Differentiation

Unfortunately, new and novel products are not created by management-generated project methodologies. My company has a project approval system that consisted of passing a number of "gates." The first gate would be to firm up the product or process concept. The next was to develop a project plan then the product or process would be demonstrated. The problems would be addressed and so on until the product was put into production. Almost all projects required inventions and they would budget two weeks for the invention; like inventing something was similar to buying a file cabinet. You show "invention needed by 12/15" in the plan and that takes care of that phase of the project. The legal criterion for an invention in the USA is that it be novel and non-obvious. It is not easy to invent. Patent applications require a search of previous patents in the area of the invention. This step usually shows that almost everything has been tried in the past.

Inventions usually come from inspirations and lots of hard work trying many iterations. My first patent (on an optical recording disk) started by cutting up paint cans in my basement along with trying scores of concepts using things I had on hand in my basement workshop. It was very difficult to do invention experiments at work because the lab where I worked did not have the tools, materials, and machinery that I had available in my home workshop.

There was next to no hand tools available because they would get pilfered or lost by employees. The company refused to require people who needed hand tools to do their job to buy their own. So, most technicians did not have the tools they needed.

The company wanted teams to invent as needed for projects. It is very difficult for a team to invent because of the differences in opinion and because team members have different levels of creativity. Teams are best used for refinement of an invention after the concept is established. The other deterrent to team invention is intellectual property theft. One time I sat in team meetings and said; why don't we try polyamide-imide as the material of construction?" Nobody at the meeting seemed to think much of my idea. However, several months later, a person who attended the meeting applied for a patent on my idea (and she got it). The point that I am trying to make with these discussions is that differentiating products cannot be produced by project plans or team meetings. It takes an idea, usually the "kernel" comes from one person and not every employee has the creativity needed to be an inventor.

> **RULE:** Do not rely on a group/team for needed inventions. It takes a spark. Enlist your top talent.

If project plans and meetings cannot produce differentiated products, what does it take? My opinion, as you can see from my exit essay, is that it requires a company department whose charge is nothing but development of new products. My first employer, then the largest corporation in the US at that time, did it right – in my opinion. They had many divisions and many product lines, but each division had a product-engineering department.

New differentiating products came from these departments. Long-term concepts were worked on in a central corporate research lab, which interfaced with the product engineering functions in the various divisions.

If a division made radios, there would be a technical staff dedicated to development of new radios that were better than the competition. The research labs might be working on computer-controlled radios or radios that are powered by a solar cell; a long-term development. This is not a weird concept, but recently I was hired to present a tutorial in my specialty for a large corporation and I learned that they also had my company's chaotic approach to product development. The research staff decides to develop a process or product that they think may be saleable, and then tries to force fit what they developed into various divisions. The divisions or customers did not ask for what they were developing and some of their major efforts were not in their area of expertise. It is appropriate to have a large range of products in a big corporation to take care of varying demands in product lines. However, that does not mean that a large automobile company should diversify by acquiring a bread bakery. Baking bread is not within their expertise. They could diversify by selling, for example, buses or recreational vehicles; products that use their engine or sheet metal expertise.

> **RULE:** If you must diversify, do it in an area
> where you have competency.

The following list contains some thoughts on steps to take to achieve product differentiation:

1. Establish a product development function (with new products as their only responsibility).

2. Staff your product development department with the best, creative talent in the organization (use demonstrated creativity accomplishments as the selection criteria).
3. Establish your differentiation goal (which product do you want to better).
4. Research the products that you want to beat.
5. Test your products to make sure that they work.
6. Test market your products and see if customers agree that they are better.
7. Do not build manufacturing facilities before test marketing a reasonable number of units.

If you can find an appropriate business school, all company officers should complete a course in "how to recognize a profitable product." I suspect that the officers of my last employer either flunked this course or they attended a course on "how to manufacture products that lose money." This course was probably designed for companies that have too much money and need to lose some for tax purposes. I have been "out" for three months now and I shake my head everyday when I see lost business opportunities, and some of the "dumb" products that the company introduces. They used to sell to people, the 5.9 billion ordinary people in the world. Now they seem to be directing their products only to the 100 million "special people" with incomes above the US mean and to unidentified businesses. The company was successful for more than one hundred years by marketing their products to all income levels.

> **RULE:** Decide to whom you want to sell.

I have saved the most important product differentiation point to last: use your products! I will never forget a product development team that I worked on some years ago. We were a team of about a dozen experienced engineers from broad backgrounds, and we were assigned the task of inventing a medical device that would only be used on women. The company hired an outside consultant, supposedly to get input from women, but there were no women on the team and not one of us will ever use what we designed. We eventually had one woman engineer assigned to the team, but a pet peeve of mine is products that just do not work. Apparently, the people who designed these products never used them. About once a month, I run into a product that "fails" when I go to use it. If it is an expensive product, I try to get satisfaction from the manufacturer, but often I do not bother, so there may be thousands of these bad products produced and sold each day and they fail, but the designer and manufacturer are oblivious because they do not use them. Recently, I purchased a new laptop computer. I am not as computer literate as I should be. Alas, I lack the patience to "play" for hours to find out how to make it do what I want. So, when I could not make it save to CD (the feature that I bought the computer for), I called the help number supplied by the manufacturer. I beeped through all the phone diversions until I reached a live person and I asked her to tell me in words, how to save a word-processing document to a writable CD. She said, "Do this, this, and that, and then try this." I said, "No, I want instructions in words." She was absolutely stumped. She could not give me a recipe. I tried again, hoping to find a company employee who knew something about the computer. The second call took over a half-hour and still no success. It appeared to me that nobody at this huge computer company (over 20B/year in sales) ever used one of their laptop computers. Of course, they were made in China and I suspect the only link between the company whose name is on the computer and the company that manufactured the computer is the purchasing department. This kind of "product development" certainly does not produce product differentiation.

I conclude this chapter with an admonition to make true product differentiation a business priority. It takes a lot of work and a proper organization to make product differentiation even possible. True product differentiation requires a significant idea. If you do not have that idea yourself, you must establish a company and an environment conducive to innovation. Finally, you need to find talent to create better products. This means staffing product engineering or the organization charged with new products with people with demonstrated ability to invent.

Chapter 4: Technical Competency

This morning's newspaper carried a story about the U.S. Immigration Service's (INS) folly in posthumously granting visas to some of the 9/11 terrorists who destroyed the World Trade Center. They characterized the INS as the hallmark of incompetence. Anybody in the U.S. who has ever had to deal with this government organization probably has their own examples of the arrogance and incompetence of this organization. They made my Russian friend's wife move to Canada for a month and later to Mexico for another month because something was wrong with her paperwork, even though she came from Russia with her husband. He could stay, but they put her through hell for a year or two and made them spend money that they did not have for a lawyer.

Incompetency is epidemic in many governments; mostly because there is no accountability to the people they are supposed to serve. Government organizations can ooze along staffed with incompetents in the United States because we customers cannot get at them. A comforter of bureaucracy insulates them. Unfortunately, manufacturing companies and businesses that need to make a profit cannot survive very long without technical competence. We are not insulated from customers. We already discussed leadership competency. It is easier to carry incompetent leaders than it is to have deficient technical competency. For example, I once had a boss who decided to retire on the job. He used to have "near heart attacks" in September and take a medical leave (in Florida of course) until spring. When he was not on medical leave, he used to come in late, leave early, and take a two-hour "bridge lunch" in the superintendent's dining room. He was technically qualified when he got the job, but when you are away from the business as much as this person, you lose your technical skills and carry only outdated information. He became technically incompetent. We had a great technical team in the department and we kept the department business intact by getting reports and projects approved when the "old man" was away. The second in command was competent and a hard worker. People who know and like their jobs are often forced to carry an incompetent manager just to keep the jobs that they like. Of course, reporting an incompetent manager to his or her manager is out of the question. You will be fired. That's the law.

> **RULE:** Never try to report an incompetent person to management. You will end your career. Use anonymous employee surveys where possible.

> **RULE:** Technical incompetence cannot be concealed.

The latter rule is based upon countless examples that I have witnessed. Everyone has gone into a store and asked a salesperson about a product or service. You know immediately if you got an "airhead." He or she will tell you something that you know to be wrong information. The usual reaction is to walk away and shop for the item elsewhere. That same thing happens in industry. If you work as a plastics engineer and somebody asks you for the use temperature limit on polybenzimidizol, you should have the answer or know immediately where to look up the answer. If you stumble on technical questions, your customers will soon become aware and they will go elsewhere for their technical information. The insidious aspect of technical incompetency in U.S. industry with the proliferation of non-technical leadership incompetent technical people can go unnoticed and do much damage to a company. I encountered a Ph.D. researcher who was serious and hard working, but he did not understand the technical requirements of the business. He would work on irrelevant projects -- technologies that did not fit the business. He was quite good at talking his non-technical managers into funding, but none of his million-dollar projects ever paid off. He did not have competency in the technologies needed by the business. He was finally fired, but I estimate that his bogus projects cost the company twenty million dollars over a ten-year period.

Similarly, researchers make their living getting patents on worthless inventions. One of my former employers used to grant a $2,000.00 bonus for simply filing a patent application. Researchers started patenting everything from the law of gravity to sunsets. The U.S. government no longer requires an invention to be useful or demonstrated. I was involved with a project where a researcher patented a particular paint thickness. He produced data that said that there was something magical about a particular thickness. We all knew that this claim was bogus, but he got the patent. Besides the $2,000.00 bonus, a typical patent costs from $20,000 to $30,000 in legal fees in addition to the researcher's time, which can cost $100.00 to $150.00 per hour. All totaled, a worthless patent probably cost my company $50,000 to $100,000. The message that we are trying to convey is that technical competency is very important to a company's success and incompetency has very, very high costs. This chapter will present our thoughts on improving technical competency so that a manufacturing company can stay in business.

We will present my exit essay on technical competency and then cover assessing competency, fostering competency and dealing with deficient competency. We will conclude with suggestions for maintaining competitive technical competency.

This essay was sent to two vice-presidents, the president and the CEO. If it got through to them, they did not reply.

Exit Essay: *Technical Competency – A View from the Factory Floor*

Business people may not agree with this, but I believe that any manufacturing company's success depends on their technology – what they know and do better than others. Fuji film is the first choice of most professional photographers because they have the best product consistency (so I have been told). Toyota has the best-selling car in the USA because they reportedly have the best reliability. Bose can charge $500 for an ordinary tabletop radio because it sounds better than most radios. These winners in their fields have technical features in their products that make them preferred by customers. They sell better; more sales mean more profit, more company success. This is a simple business concept. Unfortunately I think that the company forgot it. We do not have a technology edge over the competition.

As a member of the company's technical community for almost four decades, I have been witness to continual decline in the company's technical competency. We used to hire only the best engineers and scientists. We recruited only in the top schools in the technical fields that we needed and when I started with the company, the company only hired technical people with advanced degrees. Now the company hires based on diversity quotas. In the sixties and seventies, the company encouraged technical people to continue their education throughout their careers by attending evening courses in colleges and by active participation in professional and technical societies. Professional licensing was encouraged in the engineering community. Now the worldwide engineering division is staffed mostly with people who do not have an engineering degree and in some cases no college education. Reimbursement for evening college is almost nonexistent and there are demerits rather than rewards for participation in professional and technical societies. I had one boss who threatened me a follows: You will never get another raise from me if you continue to publish papers in technical journals. I continued to publish; he also kept his promise.

The company boasts that it now provides forty hours of training a year for every employee. The truth of the matter is that most employees expend their mandated forty hours on internal courses that have little or no substance or are not at all technical training. For example, my training this year consisted of mandated diversity school, mandated safety lectures, town meetings and a few company feel-good programs like teamwork day. Most employees have nothing in their forty–hour training program to increase the technical competence of the company's staff. This is my opinion.

Another very discouraging happening in technical competency is the flight of top young talent. I have witnessed many of our most promising young people quit for jobs elsewhere. In fact, my son recently quit. He left because he was not being challenged. We have important and challenging projects and problems to work on, but we have such a screwed up technical organization and accounting system that it is not possible to funnel the difficult and unsolvable problems to the young talent who could solve them. In addition to the young people problem, we have had twenty years of brain drain in the form of repeated retirement incentives. This has depleted the company of its senior staff and now there is none to mentor young technical staff. Essentially, the company's technology is currently below B-team status (my opinion). This is one of the root causes of our current state of distress. We do not have enough technical talent to conceive of new products and to make innovations happen.

How can the company regain its former technical competency? A first, very do-able step would be to stop staffing technical positions with non-degreed people. In fact, I recommend going back to only hiring technical people with advanced degrees in appropriate fields from accredited universities. I suggest the removal of the human resources department from all aspects of technical recruiting with exception of the paperwork. They are a contributing cause of diminishing quality in new hires. A human resources person recently told me that she only recruits women engineers and preferably only women engineers from a particular university in the Midwest of the USA. This practice is hardly selecting based upon talent and related experience. Human resource recruiters seldom understand what technical skills are needed in a particular department. Only the department staff should recruit and select new technical talent.

The company needs to develop a significant mentoring program for young talent. I was asked to mentor a young person, so I started by asking if the company had a definition of what mentoring should be. They did not even have a definition of mentoring. Maybe we should start there. On the other end of the age spectrum, the company has no succession policy. At the end of December, the company's only lubrication engineer will retire. There is nobody to take her place. We have countless critical pieces of manufacturing equipment around the world that require *lubrication and special bearings. Who will tell the operators what to do? Similar statements can be made at year-end in probably a hundred areas of company technology.*

With regard to continuing education, the company should encourage membership in technical societies and attendance at their local functions. Most societies meet about eight times per year and attendance at these meetings is usually a very effective and painless way of keeping up in a technical field. Most of these societies also have low-cost education courses. I would encourage participation by making active participation worth points on a performance appraisal. I would expect all technical people to pay for memberships and meeting costs from their personal funds, but let them be aware that raises they may get for improved performance will more than cover their personal costs.

I certainly would encourage continuing education at the university level for all employees. Again, I would only have the company pay for programs where the company needed a special skill and sent the person to school to obtain this special skill. I would review all company-training programs and delete the ones with little substance. Also, I would cancel any company training programs that compete with offerings from local educational institutions. They have professional teachers who must keep up in their field because this is the way it is in universities. They must publish or perish.

Finally, I recommend a 180-degree reversal in the company's policy of disregarding the education credentials of people selected for leadership positions in the technical community. I was told by the head of our division's leadership assessment that it makes no difference if a person in a leadership position has any formal education in the area that he or she is in charge of. This is the official company policy. The director of chemical research can be a person who spent twenty years in the dry cleaning business and only has a high school education. This is okay if he or she can handle the people. I do not think that this is a wise company policy. Managers must make important technical decisions at almost every level and the practice of putting people in leadership positions with no related formal education is, in my opinion, technology suicide.

In summary, the company has waning technical competency caused by years of misguided human resources recruiting, talent-depleting downsizings and regressive accounting practices that tie the hands of its technical staff and keep problems from getting solved. The company needs to return to hiring highly educated technical talent and put them in a system that challenges them and rewards technical successes.

Essay Reflection – Companies Need A Talent Strategy:

Essentially, my exit essay presented a shopping list of problems and a sentence or two on how I might address these problems. The items in my shopping list could probably be put into two categories: talent strategy and maintaining technical competence once technical people are hired. Having a talent strategy means deciding on what talent is needed for the business, how to get that talent, how to nurture that talent, how to retain needed talent and how to dispose of talents no longer needed. We will dedicate subsequent sections to the specifics of the strategy factors, but what we are proposing here is for top management to adopt a strategy for technical talent.

If you wish to open a restaurant, you need to decide on what types of food you will serve to differentiate your restaurant from the billions of other restaurants. You will probably pick a type of atmosphere or theme and then decide on the menu, and then you need to hire the cooking talent to make the product (customers that buy meals at a profit to you) a reality. You need to think hard about how you will find a reliable chef who is a wizard in preparing Italian (or whatever) food. You need a technical talent strategy.

My company, which has been in business for more than 100 years, did not seem to have a strategy for technical talent. Everything seemed just to happen without a plan. In the latter years of my career, operating divisions were simply specifying that they could support ten (or whatever) engineers this year. The next year, it may be eight. There was no mention of what kind of talent was needed to keep a particular business improving. I know with certainly that in some of the divisions that I did work for, the managers calling the shots on technical staff were not technical people, and there is no way that they could chart the technology path for their business. They lacked the technical competency to produce a technical strategy.

What to do? It is a fact of life in manufacturing in the U.S.A. that many managers got their positions for their "soft" skills (or sucking up). The way that this situation can be dealt with is for each manager to have a technical advisor. I saw this system work in the shop department in a division where I worked. This was a huge operation, over 1,000 machinists, skilled tool and die-makers, instrument makers and related skilled people. These people could build any machine, install it in production and make it a reliable producer of product for sale. They were exceptional, probably the best machine shop in the world.

The top manager was never a machinist. He or she was usually an engineer. I used to do a lot of consulting for the machine shop on material problems and I got to know the inner working of the organization. I learned that when the organization was at its peak in ability, results and costs, the top manager had a technical advisor who was a machining and fabrication genius. This person could run every machine in the place, know the complicated math needed to pull off difficult machining sequences, and had the ability to tell others how to make an operation come out right without insulting them. When the question arose on updating a piece of equipment, this technical advisor would to the study and make a recommendation to the manager that was always in the company's best interest. This manager had the very best technical advice. He made the right technical decisions as assessed by business profits.

My advice to non-technical managers who must make technical decisions is get yourself a technical expert that you can trust wholly and completely (not a suck-up) and make this person a part of your decision-making team. In the machine department that I brought up as a model, the technical advisor did this as a full-time job. He was called a machining technician or some such title, but his job was technical advisor to managers as well as to people running machines. It need not be a full-time job. It requires the highest technical competency, integrity and trust. This is a person that you would trust with your life. I have never been a manager, but I have always had a technical advisor in everything that I do. It works. Try it.

> **RULE:** When you make important decisions, plans or statements, seek the opinion of your trusted advisor first.

Now, if I convinced you that you should have a technical advisor, if you are not a technical expert, I want to talk you into establishing a technical strategy. Decide on the technologies that you need to differentiate you from your competition and develop a plan to get, keep and grow these technologies.

Assessing Technical Competency

The best way to assess technical competency is to be technical competent and work with the person you are assessing on a project. Most homeowners have painted a room or two. When people offered to help, you will very quickly learn who has the necessary skill and who just creates damage and extra work. If you want a successful outcome, you will have to somehow get rid of the person who lacks the necessary skills. I have put these well-intentioned people in charge of coffee and placing drop cloths.

Unfortunately, when you hire somebody off the street or out-of-college, you do not have the opportunity of personally working with this person. How do you assess the technical competency of a new hire? Since I advocate only hiring engineers and scientists with advanced degrees, you can get a reasonable assessment of technical competency by reviewing their thesis work and by discussing the candidate with his or her thesis advisor. You can supplement this input with a careful interview in which you ask questions that probe depth of understanding of concepts. For example, if you are interviewing a plastics engineer, ask him or her to tell you what they know about polyethylene or other common plastic. If you get a one-sentence reply: "It is a plastic with a monomer structure of just carbon and hydrogen," you may want to question this person's depth of knowledge. If the person goes on for five minutes and tells you more than you want to know about polyethylene – you may have a person with good technical competency. If you are wondering why I did not suggest just reviewing the person's grade point average, the simple answer is that sometimes, the smartest people cannot make projects and products happen. I have been given various summer students to mentor through the years and some of the brilliant 4.0 students were functionally incompetent. They could not produce results. Some were simply wizards with a computer; they could do nothing else. And, computers cannot manufacture a product (other than software). Certainly review college transcripts for key courses and the grades obtained in these courses. This gives quite an accurate profile of the candidate's areas of proficiency. It also shows if the person took the right courses to know the fundamentals in the technical areas where you need help.

Assessing "experienced" people takes more skill. References can be very misleading in the litigious U.S.A. If you call a laid-off engineer's last supervisor, he or she is likely to give a neutral to good assessment just to avoid liability. The interview is probably your only tool. Try to put the person at ease and attempt to form a psychological profile of the person. People cannot hide who they are and what they know when they are at ease and when their guard is down. I have spent many years associated with politicians as a committee person in a U.S. political party. Candidates for office come before local committees seeking their endorsements. They only talk for five minutes, but if you pay attention and analyze what was said, you can make a fair assessment on how well that person will meet the job requirements. Many candidates are egomaniacs. They spout off all sorts of alleged accomplishments and state how loyal they are to the party and how much they appreciate our letting him or her speak to the committee and how they love our town. This is the profile of a phony. A candidate who comes with a specific platform will be a better candidate than the former. The way that people speak lets you know something about their personality. A fast talker is aggressive. A slow talker is cautious; a halting talker may be uncertain about him or herself; a person who does not look you in the eye may be insincere. A person, who makes dumb statements, probably is.

> **RULE:** Let a person under evaluation talk. Talk is a window to his or her soul.

Of course, you must review a person's credentials, but make an attempt to get documentation of his or her accomplishments. If you are hiring an experienced scientist or engineer, ask ahead of an interview for a list of their publications or copies of major reports, etc. Reading a person's publications is even better than talking with a person in assessing what they are like and what they know.

> **RULE:** Read something that a job candidate has written.

My reviewers, without fail, detect any angry tone in my writing. I have had to rewrite an entire book to lower the anger in my words. This is only chapter four and I already had to rewrite a chapter to reduce the anger in my words. If a person does not write in a logical order, chances are he or she is not logical. If a person uses superlatives, he or she may be a phony. If there are misspelled words, or a poor use of grammar, that person may be careless. There certainly should be no errors in a document that a person is submitting for consideration for a job.

My final advice on assessing technical talent is, use your instinct. I know that an engineer who cannot build a deck, fix a furnace, or work with his or her hands will not be a hands-on problem-solving engineer. This observation has never failed.

> **RULE:** Look at the job candidate's fingernails. The best engineers have dirt/grease under them.

Similarly, if you do not like a person after an interview, you will not like that person as an employee. If there is something not quite right in his or her work history, be cautious. If there are mannerisms that annoy you, be cautious. Mothers know almost immediately if they want their child playing with another child. They have an instinct that identifies trouble. Do the same – use your instincts; they are probably right.

Fostering Competency:

Positive reinforcement promotes any behavior. Acknowledging and rewarding technical results will certainly make keeping technically up-to-date worthwhile. How can this be done? My company had a dual career path where there were various coded (and salary ranges) applied to scientist or engineer positions. An engineer could have a code higher than his or her boss and make more money than the boss. This seldom occurred, but the system existed and it did foster keeping oneself technically astute.

I am a big advocate of continuous learning. A technical person is not done when he or she finishes formal schooling. Technical people should be encouraged and rewarded for taking college courses to improve or establish a needed skill. Technical people can learn from each other by teaching each other. I read that a large hi-tech company in the U.S. had a program where technical staff has periodic meetings with one member of the department teaching the others something that he or she knows well. I tried to implement such a system, but met with failure because our accounting system would not allow us to charge the time to department burden. In my first two months of retirement, I gave tutorials on technical subjects to two of the largest chemical companies in the world. They both networked talks via computers and teleconferencing such that my talk went to their plants in various parts of the company. What a good idea. They paid me just a few hundred dollars honorarium and they achieved the results of sending scores of people to a technical conference sponsored by a technical society. Needless-to-say, I encourage this kind of teaching with your technical staff.

Probably the best way to foster technical competency is to grow a company culture that encourages continuous learning, technical excellence, and participation in technical societies and rewards this participation. The atmosphere should be like it is at most universities where pursuits in one's field are preeminent.

> **RULE:** Make technical competency part of
> company culture.

Dealing With Deficient Technical Competency:

I already discussed firing and transfer as ways to deal with deficient technical competency, but that would never happen in many companies, like the one I retired from. They often promoted technical incompetents – this is the "Peter Principal." Employees know each other and their boss. Technical competency of a manager could be rated by a properly designed annual survey. One college that I taught at did this. At an unannounced time, I received a note in my mailbox to have a student go to the information center, pick up survey forms, conduct the survey and return the forms – all during the first half hour of class. About a month later, I would receive the tabulated results from the department chair. He never commented, but of course, he reviewed the results. The questions were worded to determine technical competence as well as teaching ability. They would ask: Is the instructor well prepared for class? Does he or she know the subject? Are meaningful examples used? Are the tests insightful? Etc. There were about forty questions and without a doubt, they let the department chair know if I was technically competent enough to teach this course. This can be done in industry to rate managers. On the other hand, coworkers rating each other does not work well. They tend to go after each other and it jeopardizes teamwork. The technical competency of employees can be assessed by their accomplishments.

Deficient employees can be improved by structured improvement plans. "Unimproveable" employees need to be removed. Managers with deficient technical competency should be removed.

> **RULE:** Remove technical incompetency in critical areas.

The first big corporation that I worked for had a novel way of dealing with general managers whose divisions were operating in the red. They would send them to the corporate research center and make them "executive engineers." They had very nice offices, a secretary, and the authority to make us underlings try their ideas. Nobody but the secretary worked for these executive engineers. I was working in metal casting research at the time and one executive engineer made me try a ludicrous casting technique that did not work. Thus, they were an annoyance to the ordinary engineers, but they no longer could make a division lose money. We had three or four in the lab that I worked in. They usually voluntarily retired or left the company after a short stint as a powerless executive engineer. It was a rather humane way of getting rid of high-level managers who had deficient competency.

I do not advocate the executive engineer approach to dealing with incompetent technical staff, but assigning these people to do useful studies and special projects is often a good way to prevent them from causing costly problems and possibly get useful work from them. Sometimes, these people have talents that make them a significant company asset when they are removed from their technical roles. If they do not produce results in their non-technical assignments, they should be removed.

Summary:

This chapter came out longer than intended so we will conclude with an admonition to make technical competency a company priority and some suggestions on how to improve and maintain technical competency:

1.   Develop a metric to assess the competency of your technical staff (e.g., each person can submit on annual report of accomplishments that is reviewed by others and verified).
2.   Reassign technical staff with deficient competency.
3.   All engineers and scientists should have advanced degrees or professional licenses.

4. Establish a strategy on how to hire the best college graduates and mentor them.
5. Do not promote people without appropriate formal education to professional-level technical positions.
6. Establish a viable mentor program for new hires and reward mentors.
7. Encourage participation in technical societies.
8. Use retired technical talent for "messy" projects that require continual focus.
9. Never discriminate in hiring, promoting, or college recruiting.
10. Foster collaboration and develop a strategy and reward effective examples.
11. Teach each other.
12. Define needed competencies.
13. Bring technical staff together on a regular basis in small enough groups that they can get to know each other (e.g., presentations, symposia, etc.).
14. Require each department to have a plan to foster and maintain technical competency.

RULE: Require managers to have competency in the area that they manage.

When I retired, there were sixteen people in the engineering laboratory that I worked in. Less than half had the technical skills and education needed for the job. Many departments were in similar condition. The net effect on the corporation was visible in the marketplace and on Wall Street.

CHAPTER 5:   Marketing

Marketing is key to any business. It is also not a science. You cannot hire a Ph.D. in marketing and assume the best marketing. Some people are natural salespeople and those are the ones that you want in your marketing organization. They are usually people oriented; they like dealing with people; they are usually nice appearing people; they have a good smile; dress in style and are well groomed (as opposed to disheveled). Natural salespeople can talk "good." They remember names and faces; they take an interest in you as an individual. So marketing, first of all, needs people with these personality characteristics. They can be taught, but people do not change much, so you really want people with natural sales talent. You want people who could sell refrigerators in Antarctica and ice skates in Cancun.

I wrote an exit essay on this subject because my wife told me that my company's marketing stinks. She is probably the most qualified person in the world to make that assessment. She has been a professional shopper for the past 42 years that we have been married. She shops every day and every place we visit. She has scoured the stalls of the public market in Budapest and hit all ten floors of the Number One department store in Shanghai. And, she buys! So when she says that the company's marketing stinks, it must stink. I guess I had to concur since sales reports quantified her opinion. The company was selling less of their mainstream products each year; they were selling more of their high tech products, but these lose money, so you cannot continually sell more of money-losing products and stay in business for a long term.

I asked her what is wrong with the company's marketing. First, she said, there isn't hardly any advertising. And she should know since she watches non-cable TV every night. Secondly, when she does see an advertisement, it is lousy. "Lousy" means not memorable. She does not remember the ad or the message. So this is the problem addressed by this chapter. I will present a view from the factory floor on how manufacturing companies should market their wares. Specifically, we will discuss my exit essay, marketing ethics, the voice of the customer, marketing media and conclude with suggestions from the factory floor on how to improve marketing.

My concerns about the company's marketing were selfish. If the company doesn't sell their stuff, they cannot pay my salary and that would cause significant distress to my wife. It could alter her shopping habits. My exit essay essentially presented a shoppers view of my company's marketing. Here it is.

Exit Essay: Marketing Strategy – A View from The Factory Floor

I am not a marketing person, but I have spent forty years with a professional consumer/shopper, my wife. She watches television every night from 7 to 12 PM and knows all of the advertisements on free TV. She tells me that she seldom sees a company ad and when she does its "lousy". This means completely forgettable and often not aimed at any apparent product. She likes ads that are humorous, cute, or clever – preferably all three.

I personally observe the company's marketing in stores, outdoors advertising and in printed media. I concur with her opinion that the company's advertising is inadequate and poorly executed. About six years ago I made a trip to Japan to investigate a competitor's product line and to see if our company had any real presence in Japan. Before I made the trip, I contacted our biggest competitor's corporate headquarters and told them that I have an idea that may employ one of their technologies and I would like to see what products they have available. They replied that they would be happy to show me their products and set an appointment time for me to visit their corporate headquarters in Tokyo. I met with a vice president who spoke fluent English. He took me to an adjacent building to review their products. Each of five floors in this building was dedicated to a different product line and they had a person on each floor that knew literally everything about each of the products on their floor. Floor three contained the products that I was interested in and the woman in charge of the floor had an answer to all of my questions. All of their products were professionally displayed and all worked. When I reviewed all of their offerings and had all of my questions answered, I said "thank you" and walked out the door. I was really impressed with the effort that they made to entice a potential new customer. There was no pressure, no hype, and they did not even ask me what product I was working on. The point of this story is that I doubt that a person off the street would get a similar reception at our office. I tried many times to get product answers for other people on our products and usually got nowhere.

I can cite countless examples where I was disappointed, even embarrassed by the company's advertising. Our competitors often make our company look like a "loser". What is the problem? My wife is of the opinion that the company must have a clueless ad agency. She suggests finding an agency with a record of "winning" commercials. Secondly, advertise something specific, some benefit that our company's products have over the competition. The company's marketing director showcased his latest TV commercials at the October Engineering

Conference. My reaction to his campaign was: What the hell is he selling? I have no idea. Neither do other small business owners. Finally, please stop treating customers like dirt. As a recent high tech product customer, I have been given the "run-around" whenever I sought help in making my system work. Company sales people seem to have inadequate knowledge of the products that they sell and most are not users of the products that they sell. The company that knows how to tell the person on the street how to get into and effectively use the new high tech products will take over the market. Based upon my experiences, the company will not win the high tech market unless they make big changes. I wish there could be a company product center in major malls staffed with a person who is surrounded by examples of the company's products and with answers on any product need. Maybe these centers would not sell anything, only refer people to other mall stores that sell the company's products. They would be like the product experts that I saw in Tokyo.

In summary, the company seems to have a marketing strategy that is "same old" in our established product lines and non-existent or alien in other products and services. The company needs to develop understandable ads that sell features. They need to develop memorable ads; they need to talk with my wife and other potential customers – my opinion.

Essay Reflection – Marketing Ethics

One thing that was not addressed in my exit essay is marketing ethics. It is possible to advertise with intentions other than selling the product being advertised. It is possible to make false statements in advertising; it is possible to mislead the public. To do these things is a violation of what I call marketing ethics. My definition of marketing ethics is showing complete honesty in all statements, claims, guarantees, and advertisements. There should be no exaggeration, no false claims, no deceptive photos, no double speak, no intent to dupe the public. Why should ethics prevail in your marketing strategy? Aside from morality, people will eventually see through unethical marketing and that could end your company. In 2002, we had the largest bankruptcy in U.S. history, the Enron Corporation, and they fell because all of their communications (advertising, employee, and stockholders) were deceptive. They used unethical accounting practices; they were not forthright to stockholders and employees on earnings (or lack of them). It all fell apart when the public learned the news of what they were doing.

On a much smaller scale in the city where I live, the local politicians employ very expensive advertising campaigns to "advertise" government services like the city airport. The politicians appear in the ads, which are paid for by the electorate, to advertise the use of an airport that we have no choice in using. The county clerk is advertising the motor vehicle department with taxpayer funds. She is in the ads, which run through the year and more at election time. She is advertising the bureau of motor vehicles. There is no other place to obtain operator's license or vehicle license. Many politicians do the same. They find a "cause" to advertise with them in the ads. This gives them huge exposure not available to most opponents, and this practice is a prime example of unethical advertising. It is being done for reasons other than marketing a product or service. They market individuals at public expense.

Politics in the U.S.A. and elsewhere are not good examples of ethics, but I witnessed similar deception in my company's advertising. They were advertising a product as a universal solution to a problem when all of us who knew the product intimately knew that it would not perform as claimed in company ads. I complained in the strongest terms to the vice-president of the division responsible, and in the communication that I received as my note cascaded down the management chain, I learned the reason for the deceptive advertising. The product that this division was pushing was cheaper to make than other products that were more appropriate to do the job. They simply made more profit on the product that they were misrepresenting. This deceptive marketing was an easy way to increase profits and improve the image of the division managers. The undocumented side of this story is the countless customers who were forever lost because they bought a product that was advertised to do something that it could not. People never forget this kind of an experience, they tell their family and friends about their bad experience, and the net effect is a ten-fold loss in customers. Each disappointed customer probably produces an additional ten "forever lost" customers. When I started to tell others how I was duped by my company's ads, I found many others similarly duped and we all preached, "stay away from this product" to all who would listen. In this instance, I suspect that company managers were not the source of the ethics lapse. I believe it was engineers who duped managers. This is part of the problem with managers who do not know the business well enough.

RULE: Ethics must prevail in marketing.

Selection of Advertising Media

How a company spends its advertising dollars must depend on the "Karma and Essence" in the marketing conference room. I never worked in a marketing department, but I watched countless movies set in New York City advertising agencies. These movies usually have the star come up with a brilliant idea and he or she gets a big office and lots of money. These movies always show a campaign that involves multiple media: printed, TV, radio, special promotions, outdoor advertising, and the Internet. The problem that disturbs me is that my company seems to do none of the above. I seldom watch TV, but I cannot recall seeing any company ad within the last year or two of my employment. My wife, the shopper, told me that there are a few company ads, but they are lousy. A similar situation exists for printed media. In my 38 years with the company, I never heard a radio ad and never saw billboards. The company seems to "blow" the advertising budget on special events whose results I question. For example, they sponsor a race car that never wins. A racing team commitment costs millions of dollars annually and the exposure is limited to the small percentage of the population who go to auto races. They similarly spend many millions becoming sports event sponsors, but these are so infrequent that it is hard to imagine that they have any effect on continuous sales.

We factory workers felt that the company was not doing its marketing job and we bear the burden in layoffs and no money for capital equipment. It seems to us that the way that the company should market its products is to use the advertising media that have a proven record of producing significant results. TV is the media with the largest worldwide audience. All countries have television access; even some of the poorest countries in the world have TV accessible to most residents. So, it seems like this is the medium to concentrate on. The other media do not seem appropriate when you are trying to attract customers at all economic levels all over the world.

> **RULE:** Advertise in media that reaches all of your markets.

The Voice of the Customer

Company executives almost always used this cliché when they gave pep talks to employees. They would state that this product (which to us workers seemed like dumber than a pet rock) is what "the customers" want. I question if the company's marketing people had any idea at all of what customers like and dislike. Again, in my 38 years with the company, I never witnessed a customer survey; I never participated in one and I never heard of anyone ever being surveyed by my company. Where does the customer voice that they refer come from? I know that they continually ask employees to test products, but this certainly is not an objective study. Employees cannot view products that mean their livelihood with any objectivity. To me, they were a huge waste of time.

My wife used to participate in true voice of the customer studies. We used to have a local manufacturer of condiments and spices. This company used to solicit through word of mouth that they needed volunteers to come to the company's experimental labs to taste new products. The volunteers were paid $20.00 for an evening tasting session that lasted between one and two hours. There were about twenty volunteers at each session and these sessions were held in a pleasant conference-room atmosphere. The volunteers would be very honest and because of the money and perks, they did not mind answering a lot of questions about the product. My wife loved to go to these sessions because they made it a pleasant event (even though she gave a big "thumbs down" to their brown ketchup).

I get countless mail and phone surveys from companies asking about their products and I throw out all the mail surveys (even the ones containing a crisp dollar) and I have all my phone calls screened so that I do not have to argue with phone survey people. It is hard to get customer input. Every working person in the U.S.A. is busy to the point where he or she cannot afford to volunteer five minutes to help a survey company that is charging for their services. I believe that the only way to get an objective voice of the customer is to pay people well enough to be honest.

> **RULE:** If you want honest market survey data, pay the survey participants well.

Needless-to-say, marketing surveys need to be well designed to get the information needed. Questions need to be straightforward and not convoluted. Ask: "Do you like this product?" "Why?" "Why not?" Do not ask a convoluted question like: "If you were to consider buying this product in lieu of buying an article of personal clothing, what enhancements should we make to have you prefer to buy our product?" All of the surveys commissioned by my company were the convoluted variety. Also, beware of people reading subliminal messages in questions. People often analyze questions and give the survey author the answer that they think that they want rather than the honest answer. I'll never forget the one time that I took an inkblot test. It was administered by my company's human relations department when I started employment. We were shown about twenty inkblots and were given a selection of five responses as to what each looked like. All of the twenty groups of responses contained at least one that said that the inkblot looked like a body part. I deduced that if you checked that one, they would label me a sex fiend or cannibal. So, I never checked any body parts. When the Ph.D. psychologist interviewed me after the test, she told me that she knew that I was a homosexual. Apparently, I was supposed to check off a few body parts to be heterosexual.

The very best way to get a valid voice of the customer is to ask people in normal settings what they like and dislike about a product. When the subject of barbecue grills comes up at a cocktail party, and you design barbecue grills, do not tell the gathered people and quiz them about brands, features, problems, etc. If you are in marketing or a product designer, this should be standard operating procedure.

> **RULE:** Gather marketing information anonymously in social settings.

Summary – How to Market Consumer Products

The element of marketing that must be of highest priority is ethics. Ads must be truthful and not misleading. Remember that false claims always, always, come around to injure business. Advertising should stress documented product differentiation.

> **RULE:** If you do not have true differentiation to market – get some.

Advertising should be directed to the world. Just about any manufacturing business needs to sell to the world to be competitive. You may invest more efforts in certain countries, but worldwide marketing is essential to existence. Your local market may be dormant, but the Far

East market could be booming. Worldwide marketing can help bridge economy swings.

> **RULE:** Sell at all times and sell to the world.

> **RULE:** Only use advertising media with documented results.

Honest customer feedback can be difficult to obtain. You still must attempt to get customer reaction in any way possible. By all means, use your company's products. If you sell Fords, drive a Ford. If you sell diet pills, take them yourself or have a trusted family member use them. This will provide excellent feedback on how good your products are. I bought a battery operated trim saw this week. I used it to cut thin sheets of plywood to length. Total cutting time was less than ten minutes. I got a blister from the safety button that I had to depress at the same time as I depressed the trigger. If the designers of this product ever used it, they would very quickly learn that the safety button needed a weaker spring and it should have been molded from a forgiving material such as thermoplastic elastomer rather than a sharp-edge rigid plastic.

> **RULE:** Use what you sell – all the time.

Find out what customers want by test marketing prototypes and interviewing big users of existing products. Send products to people and ask them to use them. Loan new products to potential customers and have them use them.

> **RULE:** Promote test drives and get feedback.

My final suggestion on how to market products is to seek every opportunity possible to sell. Sell to coworkers, sell to friends, sell when you are on vacation, sell at church socials. Never stop selling and make all of your employees marketers. However, you can only do these things if you have a good product.

> **RULE:** All employees must get out there and sell.

CHAPTER 6:   Purchasing Practices

Somewhere in the size evolution of a company, it becomes necessary to initiate a purchasing department. In mom and pop operations, mom or pop does all of the buying. Buying feed stocks and equipment for any business can be a significant job. It takes time to find suppliers, screen them, evaluate prices and delivery and take care of the logistics of buying and paying for the purchases. Purchasing departments take care of all of these details and free manufacturing managers from the work required to get the materials and services needed to run a manufacturing company. In other words, a purchasing function is an essential part of most companies. What is the problem? In my opinion, the purchasing department of my former company became a part of their shortfall in business success. They developed a lapse in ethics over the past twenty years or so. Suppliers are not happy with our business practices. Employees feel frustrated because they cannot get their tasks accomplished because of purchasing impediments and products have developed "problems" because purchasing tries to redesign them through purchasing practices rather than engineering.

The purpose of this chapter is to point out how purchasing practices can affect business success and to present a view from the factory floor on how purchasing departments should operate. The objective of this chapter is purchasing philosophies that have business ethics and respect for suppliers as cornerstones. Two examples of unethical purchasing practices that are probably widespread in U.S. industry are making employees loan the company money for business travel and late payment of suppliers. My company started mandatory employee loans with no interest in the early 1990's, maybe the 1980's. When we used to travel on company business, we used to be given tickets by the company travel department and a cash advance to cover our out-of-pocket expenses such as meals, hotel, and car rental. In the new system, the people who need to travel were given charge cards paid for by the company, but in our names. If we were taking a trip, we would order airline tickets from a designated supplier and the supplier would simply put the tickets on the charge card in our name. So, if we were flying to California a month from now, we may see the ticket charge on the charge bill that arrived in the next day's mail. It would have to be paid within 30 days, but remuneration from the company, which might take from 30 to 60 days after application for remuneration. The net effect of this system was thousands of employees loaning the company money and the company paid us no interest. The year before I left, the plot thickened. They mandated that all expense accounts be submitted in digital form on the computer. The software that the company bought was cleverly designed to make the submission of an expense account so complicated and frustrating and, just plain ridiculous, that nobody wants to travel, much less turn an expense account. A friend of mine printed out the instructions. It took over 100 pages. I spent four hours with a tutor trying to input a $97.00 claim for a visit to a vendor and this was after the third time that I tried to get it to work by myself. I decided that my health was more important than the money. The company still owes me for a trip to Grimsby, Ontario and another to Philadelphia, PA.

The company does not pay suppliers in a timely manner. This scheme is another profound example of unethical purchasing practices. Big U.S. companies feel that they are the plums of the business world. If you are a Microsoft-type company, every supplier wants to be your supplier. Because of this, you can dictate payment terms. Well, my company and lots of the U.S. giants, dictate that they will not pay for supplies or services until 60 days after receipt. The big corporations are essentially asking their suppliers to loan them money (the cost of the goods or services) interest free, for thirty days past the 30-days that is normal in ethical business practices. Suppliers have told me that the situation is even worse with my old company. One time a supplier refused to quote on an instrument that I wanted to buy because my company still had not paid for the last "sale" that he made to the company.

I believe this practice to be widespread. I have been retired for four months. In that time, I did consulting for two top companies in the world in a particular business. It took me four hours of phone calls and three months to get paid by the first, and I am in month number three waiting to get paid by the second. Needless-to-say, these kinds of purchasing practices are unethical. I believe them to be dishonest. They save the company money because they use other's money. It is a forced use of the employees' or suppliers' money. We are losing the earning power of that money. Big companies are bullying money from "weaker" companies and individuals.

> **RULE:** Never intentionally delay payments due. It's stealing.

This chapter will discuss my exit essay on purchasing and then discuss the ethics of supplier relations, purchasing bureaucracies, and the technical aspects of purchasing. We will conclude this chapter with suggestions on how to partner rather then pressure suppliers.

Purchasing Issues

Dishonesty camouflaged as a business model is not the only purchasing problem that filtered down to the factory floor. My exit essay summarizes my feelings at the time.

Exit Essay: **Purchasing – A View from the Factory Floor**

I assume that purchasing departments were invented to reduce costs in large businesses. Consolidating similar purchases from various divisions allows quantity discounts. Thus a purchasing department is a good concept. Currently, within the company nothing can be bought or even discussed with a supplier without a purchasing agent being involved. I recently needed a box of special screws costing about $25 and it involved hours of phone calls to find a screw buyer and several more hours of negotiations to arrive at a supplier. Then the supplier was not on the company's approved list so there was a two-week approval delay. Then I had to have the screws sent to a mailbox that I rented because there is a better than 80% chance that a small parcel will be lost in the purchasing department's package delivery system. Forgive my negative tone; last year the receiving department lost a small package sent to me that contained $80,000 worth of proprietary tooling and I had to absorb this cost in my project. So our purchasing seems to me to be too complex, and I am less than pleased with their receiving system. Other issues that I think need to be addressed are:

1. *Inadequate technical competency of purchasing agents*
2. *Supplier approval is carried to unnecessary extremes*

3. *Purchasing agents cross the line and re-engineer products*

The following are my opinions on solving these perceived problems.

Purchasing agent competency – In the old days, a purchasing agent knew just about everything about the commodities that he or she was buying. Working in the metallurgical laboratory, I had frequent communications with the company's metals buyers. We were on various teams together and we relied on these buyers to find special metals to solve problems. As the metals buyers aged and retired, this 25M$/year commodity was assigned to people who had no knowledge of metals or metal suppliers. Similar changes happened in most commodities. Purchasing agents were moved about frequently so that they did not "build allegiance" with favorite suppliers.

The philosophy that purchasing agents do not need to know much about what they are buying may work on paper, but here on the factory floor, I have witnessed many instances where this philosophy cost the company a significant amount of money. For example, earlier this year the consumer product department experienced a rash of premature bearing failures on some production machines. These failures shut down manufacturing and cost the company lots of money for machine teardowns. After significant detective work, the root cause of the failures was traced to the purchasing agent changing bearing suppliers to save money without an engineering change notice. The bearings from the new supplier had different tolerances than the bearings specified by the design and they would not work in the production machines.

Approval of suppliers - The concept of reducing the number of suppliers that a company has probably comes from some business model. I am not familiar with this model, but I guess that it saves postage and check-writing costs. The harmful effect that I see here on the factory floor is that it creates a huge cost. The box of #6M x 6 socket head cap screws that I needed cost the company about six hours of my time (at $90/h) plus 30 minutes in a team meeting with nine engineers present, plus an estimated two hours of time spent by the purchasing department in handling suppler approval paperwork. Thus my $25 box of screws probably cost the company more that $1100 in addition to the cost of the purchase order and the screws. Many laboratory people and engineers continually need small purchases from new suppliers. We need things fast to solve problems. I doubt that the supplier approval system was meant for the small supplies that technical people need for studies and experiments. This program appears to add huge costs to our work and makes timely solution of many problems almost impossible. I suspect that the company could outsource purchasing of miscellaneous supplies and non-capital equipment to a service provider that will not require all of the approvals and paperwork that the company's current purchasing system requires.

Design changes by purchasing agent - the bearing example illustrates how purchasing agents can unwittingly re-engineer a piece of equipment or a product. Spare parts for production machinery, product feedstocks, and outsourced manufacturing are areas where a purchasing substitution can have disastrous results. If it were my business, I would require a formal Engineering Change Notice (ECN) on any supplier or specification change. Purchasing agents do not have knowledge of the effects of changing critical suppliers, but people in the business units should have this knowledge. I am suggesting that each business unit have a team that continually looks for low-

*cost feedstock and materials needed in manufacturing.
This team could include a representative of the purchasing
department and the team would institute a formal ECN and
get approval of all concerned before making a change for
lower cost or better quality (or both).*

*In summary, I think that the company's purchasing
department should use a staff of graduate engineers when
buying technical commodities and product feedstocks.
Purchasing agents should be required (by their
performance appraisal) to learn the technical aspects of
their assigned commodities and similarly be very informed
about suppliers in their commodity areas. The nickel and
dime items that need to be purchased should be outsourced
to a service provider. Continual cost reduction can be
enforced on important commodities and product feedstocks
by requiring every business unit to regularly demonstrate
that they have a viable purchasing/business unit team that
produces results in the form of continually reduced
purchased material costs. These are my opinions.*

The reply that I got to this essay from the corporate director
of purchasing stated that I am in no position to question
purchasing department practices. It is none of my business
how he runs his function and he implied I should be fired
for challenging his practices. As an aside, this purchasing
director was recently hired from a company with a
significantly different business. I think that he was hired as
a "hatchet-man" to reduce material costs period. The
rationale in his hiring is that he would have no allegiances
to any existing suppliers or purchasing staff. This being the
case, he would transfer all material purchases to the lowest
cost supplier and he would have no qualms about laying off
purchasing agents that he did not know.

I was involved with one of his lower cost initiatives shortly before I retired. For seventy years, the company purchased a key feed stock from a company that used to be a company division. In one of the "dark times" in the 1990's, this division (the crown jewel of the corporation, in my opinion) was spun off. Now, they are just a supplier to the corporation. Rumor has it that he was unsuccessful in negotiating lower feed stock costs so he decided to exert pressure by going to an untried supplier in another country. He "snuck" 10% foreign feedstock into production, then 20% and then waited for reaction. Nothing happened in some product lines, but some developed strange unexplained product problems – problems in the hands of customers. I retired before the product problems were solved, but without a doubt, the addition of this new feedstock altered physical properties of the product and I know this to be fact because I measured them.

The point that I wish to make clear is that there are nuances to every commodity. Each company's product is different even though it is bought as the same commodity. Many restaurants make onion soup; probably all are significantly different. I, personally, like to check out the chili at ski resorts. I have eaten chili at countless ski resorts and I can state with 100% certainty that no two were identical – yet they were all sold as "chili". Steel, cotton, pulp, calcium chloride, just about any feedstock is slightly different from different suppliers and these differences can bite you.

> **RULE:** Feedstocks from different suppliers are
> different.

Our purchasing director was testing ethics when he made this test run. The word on the floor was that he was only making a trial purchase from a new supplier to pressure the supplier that we relied on for seventy years. He was not exactly working in partner mode and the company probably paid a huge price in lost customers. Those of us who worked on the product problems produced by the new feedstock were told that we were being threatened by one of our largest customers in Japan. If the problem was not solved in a timely manner (30 days), they will not do business with us anymore. When I retired, the problem had not been solved even though a significant number of technical staff had worked on the problem for more than a year. These kinds of bullying business practices have an uncanny way of coming back at you. Honest negotiations may have lowered the price without the risk and testing costs that are inevitable in a feed stock switch.

Purchasing Bureaucracies

I mentioned the purchasing of travel services morass in the introduction of my exit essay alluded to the extra cost problem with buying only from approved suppliers. This chapter will discuss other aspects of purchasing department bureaucracies; things that they do that do not add value to a product or service. What does a purchasing department in a large organization do that may not need to be done? How can purchasing costs be reduced?

The prevailing business model appears to be consolidation of purchasing services and suppliers and long-term contracts to save costs. Over the past fifty years or so, suburbs have surrounded many U.S. cities. Cities have been getting smaller in size; suburbs have continually increased in size. The cities remain the hub of a metroplex, but they do not have the funds to be a cornerstone infrastructure. Consolidation of city and town purchasing functions is a common way of allegedly reducing costs. This same kind of consolidation is rampant in multi-unit businesses and industries. The U.S.A.'s accounting watchdogs –the General Services Organization – conducted a purchasing study in 2002. This organization suggests that combined purchasing may not lower costs at all. In fact, it increased costs for the U.S. government for many commodities. The study compared hospitals that bought through an umbrella purchasing organization that did the buying for many hospitals with hospitals that bought supplies and services by themselves.

I did not read the study, only a newspaper account, but it seems to me that somebody at a hospital must be responsible for buying syringes and somebody at the combined buying company must be responsible for buying syringes so the cost of the person at the buying company must be added to the cost of the syringes. The buying company is an extra level of bureaucracy. The combined buying model only works if the combined buyer gets costs reduced enough to pay for their organization and to pass savings along to the customer organization, the hospital.

I was involved with one of these combined buying exercises at my company. The company has manufacturing plants in ten countries and all of them buy metal -- some for products, some for building buildings and equipment. The company appointed a person from within the purchasing department to be the worldwide metal buyer. She was to negotiate contracts with a few metal suppliers and cut our metal costs in half. We had lots of meetings up front to strategize and I never heard anymore about this cost-reducing combined purchasing plan. Word here on the factory floor is that we bought such "piddling" amounts of various metals in most cases that it was not possible to get any discounts by combining. Also, some vendors did not even want the extra paperwork and hassles of supplying costs of steel to 10 different countries; they said that they simply did not want our business.

> **RULE:** Do not bully suppliers -- it can
> backfire.

The other cornerstone of purchasing consolidation, reducing the number of suppliers, never seemed to me to produce savings. Maybe they do on paper, but somebody had to pay for the huge flatbed truck that I used to see on the plant grounds carrying a load of two sixteen-foot two-by-fours. A local lumber company had an annual contract to supply our plant with dimensional lumber. It was only used for repairs and construction projects, so it could not amount to much volume. I suspect that those two-by-fours cost $100.00 each. Is this cost effective purchasing? Not in my opinion. This business model assumes that it is costly to deal with ten lumber companies every time that you need a two-by-four. However, is it fair to keep nine companies from getting any business from the largest business in town? Certainly the only fair purchasing practice would be to require notifying all lumber companies to bid on the annual contract.

> **RULE:** Let all suppliers who want to, bid on annual
> contracts.

With regard to establishing preferred suppliers, I do not know the details of how my company "approved" suppliers, but anything less than a system open to all would be unfair and unfair practices usually do not save money in the long term. It is common knowledge that large companies and municipalities in the U.S.A. have programs that essentially dictate that "minority" companies shall get business over all others. Of course this is not fair; this is not good business; this is not ethical or honest to stockholders. As an example of how these unethical practices can go awry, my company financed an African-American employee's attempt to be a preferred supplier.

He was a company employee and he retired to start a business to supply the company with wooden skids for a particular division. The company somehow assisted in the financing of this "minority" supplier and the business started to make skids and supply the company. According to the newspaper account, after a year or two, the minority company started to fail in meeting delivery of skids and the company tried to move the business to another supplier. The net result was a very fat discrimination lawsuit that undoubtedly cost the company a large amount of money.

> **RULE:** Do not choose suppliers on birth circumstance or other non-business measures.

Now that I am a potential company supplier (of consulting services), I want to be able to contact the purchasing department and have my list of services posted on some sort of computer base that is searched by a non-biased piece of software. When somebody calls the company purchasing department and requests analytical testing, I want my company name to come up on the screen as a candidate supplier. Then I want the purchasing agent to review the "detail" screens on each supplier and then the purchasing department should select the first supplier to contact based on the best fit of listed services to the purchase order needs. I would then like to get a call from the purchasing agent and have a fair chance of getting the work. And this is how purchasing departments should select suppliers.

> **RULE:** Open your business to all qualified suppliers.

Technical Support

As implied in my exit essay, I had many purchasing problems that arose from the lack of technical expertise on the part of purchasing agents. When the purchasing department allowed people to purchase a particular commodity for a number of years, he or she developed enough knowledge to be helpful to us when we were buying a particular supply or piece of capital equipment. On supplies, they knew when a change required engineering intervention. On supplies, they knew how to write contracts to ensure that work got done in a timely manner and how to ensure warranty of the work. On capital equipment, they knew how to make us check compatibility of motors and electrical devices with the factory electrical systems. They knew about the risks of using electrical devices made in countries with different electrical standards. They knew about codes that we must conform to for safety or environmental reasons. More is required of a purchasing person than knowing how to use the phone and writing purchase orders.

> **RULE:** Require that purchasing agents have skills or knowledge in the commodity that they buy.

My worst experience with an unqualified purchasing agent involved buying a key feed stock for a key product. This person again was a "minority" by company definition and those of us who had to deal with her knew that she was given the position because of her birth circumstance. As a team, we tried valiantly to "carry her," but she screwed up so many things and was so abrasive to our single-source supplier that at one meeting she so incensed the president of the supplier company that he said that he did not want our business and we can find another supplier. Somehow a purchasing department manager smoothed things over and the problem purchasing agent was assigned to less critical commodities, but eventually, she caused other problems that essentially necessitated giving her a "medical retirement" (at age 40). This lapse of ethics in giving an unqualified person a job cost the company dearly.

If I had a big company, I would hire a metallurgist to buy steel, a chemist to buy chemicals, a computer scientist to buy computers, an accountant to purchase accounting services, and industrial engineer to purchase building services, a dietician to buy cafeteria services, an electrical engineer to buy electronics, a mechanical engineer to buy capital machines and a chemical engineer to buy processing equipment and piping. I would demand buyers of an item to have training knowledge and skills in their area of responsibility. I would require that purchasing agents have technical competency in what they are buying. This is the only strategy that makes business sense to me.

Summary

I worked closely with many purchasing agents over the years and most were well qualified to do the job that they were in. However, over the last decade, it became the practice at my company and probably many U.S. companies to use the purchasing departments as a way to create white-collar positions for minorities who were not qualified for manufacturing or technical positions and to adopt the strategy that purchasing agents should change commodities frequently. They also seem to disregard ethics in supplier relations. The following are my suggestions on how to restore ethics to the task of purchasing supplies and services to run a business, organization, or municipality.

1.   Establish a purchasing code of ethics and use it.

2. Establish a system to give equal opportunity for any business to become a supplier.
3. Cut bureaucracy and simplify purchasing procedures.
4. Do not use the purchasing department as a collection point for employees that are not working out elsewhere.
5. Make purchasing a company technology – teach agents how to do it right.
6. Develop a continual cost reduction strategy that does not bully suppliers.
7. Treat suppliers as business partners.
8. Do not change suppliers on feedstocks without engineering approval.
9. Do not discriminate in staffing.
10. Hire only qualified people.

CHAPTER 7:   Accounting Practices

The Problem

The recent bankruptcy of Enron and other huge American corporations point out fundamental weakness in U.S. corporations: Nobody is watching the people counting the money. I have spent forty-three years working for some of the largest corporations in the world and I have never met a company accountant or even knew a person who knew a corporate accountant. Who does this work? Who collects receivables? Who borrows money? Who orders stock sales? Who determines how much to spend on research and development? Who determines how much to spend on capital? Who determines maximum pay for various positions? Who collects data for the annual report? Who pays the taxes?

I have no idea, and I suspect that 99.9999 percent of all manufacturing employees in the U.S.A. feel the same. Accounting in U.S. industry is a black hole. Are there people with CPA credentials doing this work? Or is it being done by people who have no formal accounting education, but can input data fast. Any time that there is a function in a corporation that is exempt from scrutiny of stockholders, there is a risk of illegal or incompetent behaviors that could have a negative effect on the business. The major problem addressed in this chapter is general distrust of corporate accounting practices and the problems produced by incomprehensible technology funding. Ordinary employees know how most things work in their company with the exception of accounting. When we read the annual report, we invariably see one or more "zingers" put in to make income meet expenses. These are things such as "restructuring allowance" that can mean anything and be made any number. If the person on the street (we stockholders) cannot understand the figures, they are not properly presented.

RULE: Present annual results in a manner that can be understood by <u>all</u> who are likely to read the annual report.

I suspect that cosmic arithmetic of monies pervades annual reports in most U.S. corporations. In fact, one time I requested the annual reports of government authority that sells hydroelectric power to others and after I read them, my reaction was: Why weren't the politically-approved managers of the authority in jail for grand theft from the state's taxpayers? Technology funding may not be as pervasive as the cosmic arithmetic that we see in annual reports, but it sure was a critical problem with my company. We never seemed to fund the business, but there were always lots of funds for projects not associated with the business: planting shrubs, tearing down good buildings, sponsoring racing teams, even illegal political campaign contributions – things that challenge ethics and common sense.

This chapter will start with a discussion of my exit essay on accounting and follow with some thoughts from the factory floor on capital versus business expense and how accounting should work. The objective of this chapter is more open and truthful accounting practices and accounting systems that promote rather than subvert the business.

Technology Funding

Being in engineering for my entire industrial career, I have had to continually contend with procuring funding for projects. When I started in engineering, it was easy. The boss told me what to work on and he checked on me regularly to make sure that I was working on what he wanted me to work on and if I was producing the results expected within the expected schedule. I did not have to worry about funding. The projects assigned to me came with funding and my costs were distributed to the products coming out the door of the factory. I understood the accounting system. The plant that I worked in was only one of a hundred or so plants in the corporation, but they all took the cost of a plant's technical staff and prorated it on the products out the door of that particular plant. If you had a job, you were funded and you worked on what managers asked you to work on. My last job started out with a similar system, but in 1970 or so the accountants decided that the engineers needed to be paid for by just the production departments that needed engineers. So each week we would take our 40 hours and distribute them to the departments who we felt benefited from our work. We had a list of maybe 200 departments to choose from. Then they added a system to fund big projects. We would write a project proposal or have a project assigned by a manager and this would give us funds to pay for our time as well as the funds obtained by performing small jobs for various departments. Then they went to a system where a department requesting work had to supply us a charge number and big projects were funded by a score of platforms, which meant lump funds were given to about ten managers and we had to write proposals to these platform managers to obtain funding. Finally, they did away with the technology leaders with funds and made it virtually impossible to get substantial funding from production departments. How did we function under this system? I retired. I could see no way that I could get funding to cover the 1728 hours that I had to charge to others at a rate of $90.00/hour.

> **RULE:** If you pay a technical staff, use it.

I guess that this was the accountant's goal – produce an impossible funding situation and make the technical staff quit or retire. It worked, but I do not think that it is good business practice to create an anti-technologist environment in a business that only exists because it has technology that others do not. Many corporations consider their technical staff to be part of their intellectual property and they protect their intellectual property by retaining technical staff and trimming everything else. Here is my exit essay that gave specifics to our executive committee on this subject.

Exit Essay: *Corporate Accounting Practices – A View from the Factory Floor*

Most company employees at my level have no idea of the accounting practices that the company uses to satisfy creditors, customers, the government, and Wall Street, but we understand quarterly profits and cash on hand. I believe the latter to be below safe levels. I have stated in prior essays what I think the company needs to do about low profits: Fix our products and learn how to market them. It is the purpose of this essay to address the accounting morass that I think is crippling the company's technical community and manufacturing units. The charge number system must be fixed if the company is to survive.

Myself, and countless others, have maintained for decades that the ridiculously complex accounting system that we must deal with here on the factory floor probably doubles the cost of everything and keeps us from solving the technology problems that are sinking the company. When I started at the company in the sixties, my boss assigned me to the various engineering projects that he wanted me to work on. I worked on these projects until they were completed to his satisfaction and he assigned new ones. Later we were asked to fill out a weekly sheet that showed the identification number of the departments that we worked for that week. We did not have to get department approval for the work. Then we moved to funding from profits; projects were funded by experimental work orders (EWO's). We were given projects with budgets for the year and we charged our time to these project numbers each week. Last year our engineering department received no EWO funding. We were told to solicit work from business units and that we must have an approved work order from a business unit or another department's EWO. Typically, I bill my 40 hours each week to from 15 to 25 different charge numbers. I have to research problems at home because business units do not want to pay for research or even reports; they only want an answer. I worked on two very large problems this year that were never solved because we did not have the charge numbers to solve these problems.

In the first problem, a team of about 20 technical people was established and it contained people from maybe ten different technical groups. We were given two weeks to identify the root cause and to present a plan the fix the problem. After six months, the problem was still not solved, but the business unit closed the charge numbers and we were told to stop working on the problem. It was not solved, but solving the problem was costing too much money. The second problem was similar, it also has not been solved, and we were told to stop working on it because there is no money to pay for the work.

There are countless other examples like the problems mentioned where the company's charge number system is hindering solutions to business problems and new *products. We have the people and skills, but cannot work on what needs to be worked on because the budget numbers will not allow it. On the other hand, there are always adequate charge numbers for burden-type activities.*

Charge numbers are well intentioned. Managers wanted to prevent people from spending forty hours on a job that could be done in four hours. However, the cost accountants have usurped managers of their decision-making role and now budget numbers, rather than managers controlling what gets worked on. We cannot fix product problems because there are no funds in department budgets to accommodate unforeseen technical problems. When activity is funded by capital projects, the charge number seems to serve as a reasonable method for cost control. However, with unanticipated problems or experimental work, the charge number system seems to break down. If the company's founder were still in charge, I suspect that he would have an accounting system that allows the solving of customer product problems. He would know the business well enough to know how much to budget for capital projects. He would budget some money from profits for R&D and new product development and he would keep a daily watch on manufacturing costs. Unforeseen problems like product problems would be funded by a 10% contingency account intended for these sorts of events. He would use managers to ensure that technical and support staff work on the right things with the appropriate amount of effort. He would replace managers who did not perform to expectations in these budget areas. He would not have an army of accountants trying to control what managers should control.

In summary, I think that the company is unnecessarily incurring significant costs for accounting practices that produce no value, and in many cases, prevent full utilization of employees and solving of important problems. We have the work; we have the staff, but the accounting system keeps employees who are already on the payroll from doing the work. I think that the founder would not tolerate such a system. The system needs to be simplified and managers should be the watchdogs of costs, not accountants - my opinion.

Surprisingly, I received an answer from the company comptroller saying that I raised some "interesting points, "but they were not about to change anything. At least it was polite.

Capital Versus Expense

My company's handling of capital and expense items made it clear to me that ethics was not a significant consideration in accounting practices. I will never forget as long as I live, the first time that I was asked to study a corrosion problem in the sulfuric acid plant. The specific incident that I was called in on was a leak in a sixteen-inch diameter pipe that ran outside of the building and carried 104 % sulfuric acid (oleum) to tankage. The pipe was made from carbon steel and the department tried to stem a leak into the soil along side of the building by wrapping the elbow with duct tape. Everyone who has ever taken high school chemistry knows that sulfuric acid dissolves carbon steel. I will spare you the details, but essentially, the plant manager knew that almost all of his piping will be corroded through within a year and he replaced it each year as a maintenance expense. He and the accountants knew that annual repair of these corroded-through systems would show up on the ledger as a tax deductible expense and if he replaced the piping with special stainless steel that would not corrode through each year, the company would have to make a capital investment and write off the cost over a number of years, maybe ten.

The accountants and manager were using the system to save money while ignoring the ethics of injuring employees by leaking acid on them and leaking untold amounts of acid into the aquifer (it does not evaporate).

> **RULE:** Being cheap can be costly in the long run.

Another questionable accounting practice was the use of R&D dollars for capital equipment and repairs. Since 1990 or thereabouts, company managers had a portion of their salary depend on meeting their accountant-dictated budgets. They would sell their own mother to slavery in a cold country to keep from overrunning a budget. They were rewarded even more for under-running their budget. The net result of this practice was no capital spending and no maintenance spending. But things break. They fixed things with R&D funding and titled it a machine improvement. Many times equipment was purchased as part of an R&D program, but it was never disposed of when the program ended. Every R&D manager knows the rules. Since the U.S. government has no staff to investigate the zillion of R&D purchases that happen each year, the company accountants and some managers forget ethics and acquire capital equipment without the delayed depreciation mandated by U.S. tax laws.

> **RULE:** Reward fiscal responsibility, not absence of spending.

One of the most flagrant accounting practices used in U.S. industry is to make capital purchases by buying a machine in pieces that cost less than $2,500. My company's definition of a capital item was something costing more than $2,500. Purchased items that cost less than $2,500 were expensed and they would be deducted from the corporate income taxes that year. They were not depreciated over a number of years. Many people in industry buy $4000.00 machines by ordering the machine base on one $2,300.00 purchase order and the drive mechanism on a separate $1,700.00 purchase order. Both items can be expensed and depreciation is avoided. The company saves money.

Many managers in my company were so tight they squeaked. I overheard some bragging about how old their cars were. I knew a manager who used to take home the coffee cans from the coffee concession. I asked him what he did with two or three large coffee cans a day. He said that he flattens them and was using them as shingles for his vacation cabin. Some used to take home toilet paper. It almost seemed like frugality to obsession was a prerequisite to become a company manager. Overall, the company rewarded not spending money and managers and their accountants bent tax laws and violated ethics to keep costs for new equipment and maintenance to zero.

> **RULE:** Do not make obsessive frugality a
> prerequisite for management.

How It Should Be

I buy my sailboat, my house and my workshop at least one new capital item each year. This year, I bought the boat a global positioning system. I bought the house a fancy light post; I bought the workshop a new planer. My stuff is up-to-date and I have learned that continual capital upgrades keep up and enhance the value of the house, boat and workshop. I have had five sailboats over my fifty years on the water, I have made money on the four that I sold because I never neglected maintenance, and I made capital improvements each year. The same situation exists in my houses. I have sold three and made money on all. I will never sell my tools, but my three sons lust for the day that I die and leave them my tools. What I am suggesting is a way of life of continual improvement and mandatory maintenance. When something gets shabby, fix it up. When something breaks, fix it properly or replace it. Of course it costs money for my annual capital purchases and for maintenance, but I budget for these things.

> **RULE:** Things break – budget for maintenance. New equipment can improve the business – budget for it.

The most unfathomable accounting practice in my company was to not fund its technical staff. Here is my reasoning. The company has 1000 engineers. Each costs the company $100,000. All engineers worth their salt save two times their salary per year in process improvements, new products, material substitutes and the like. So if you tell the technical staff to improve the business, they will net the company 200 million dollars in savings per year. However, if you maintain a technical staff and do not let them work on products or problems by withholding funding, it costs the company 100 million dollars and nothing is improved or developed. In my simple understanding of accounting, the balance sheet will show a liability of 100 million dollars for salaries of technical staff and production/product costs will be the same or the same plus inflation. If the technical staff were allowed to do their job, costs would be reduced 200 million dollars or more. It seems to me that utilization of technical staff improves business results.

When I started in engineering, we had business cycles. The U.S.A. has always had business cycles. What do you do when you have 1,000 engineers on staff and sales are down? The company that I started with always layed off production staff first. The technical staff was layed off last and all workers were given the opportunity to return when things improved. The technical staff, especially cooperative engineering students were considered to be the core of the division. We were the business. We made the business happen. My last employer never layed off people for business reasons. They were always fired. Employees understand business cycles. Production workers and technical staff would not mind a temporary layoff during business lows. Why the accountants insisted on firing staff in downturns is beyond me. If I were in charge of a big company, I would hold on to technical staff above all others. I would lay off people as necessary and not fire them.

If I were a big company, I would make ethics in accounting a mandate. I would do away with using R&D expenses for maintenance and capital purchases. I would reward business growth and process modernization instead of miserliness. I would mandate continual improvement in manufacturing equipment and products. I would obey the tax laws. I would adapt accounting procedures that are clear, crisp, open and understandable by employees and company shareowners. I would have employee auditors who could communicate to us on the factory floor what is happening in the company financial circles. I would develop a way to quantify technical staff contributions so that work in various technologies could be synergetic with business goals. I would insist on accurate production planning and marketing information to determine budgets. I would initiate a program to make employees aware of the company's finances. I would make budgeting and compensation an open process – not a backroom process. I would establish a way to turn business goals into technology funding. I would change the charging systems to return dignity to technical staff. They would not have to grovel each year for funding. Managers would be responsible for seeing that each employee in their charge was funded for as long as they are in their department. Too bad I was not in charge of my company.

CHAPTER 8:   Corporate Cultures

"Corporate culture" is a management consultant term coined to sell "get better" programs to struggling companies – my opinion. I never heard the term until my company hired a consultant in the 1980's to improve business results by changing our behaviors. They gave us lectures on culture change and every employee was given a booklet from the consulting company. It contained about a dozen ways that we must change – for example:

"Shed company loyalty and pursue aloyalty." I am not sure that aloyalty is a word, but they claimed that it is inappropriate for us employees to expect rewards for long-term service, perfect attendance, and following company rules. Liking anything from the past is loyalty to an outmoded culture. We need to change to a new culture that does not have any traditions that inhibit out continual change.

Loyalty to me meant liking the company's products, using them and promoting their use to others. I guess that this is now wrong; we should buy the competition's product and tell others to do likewise. I guess that I am not educated enough on what is the right thing to do these days. Some of the other culture changes advocated to us were:

"Make more mistakes – that is the only way to learn"
"Take risks – that is the only way to innovate"
"Go faster – the world is changing rapidly and we must adapt"
"Take initiative – do not wait for someone to tell you to solve a problem"

"Spend your energy on solutions – do not
overanalyze
problems"

The purpose of this chapter is to discuss corporate culture
from the victim's aspect. How I felt about the changes and
to suggest some ways to ascent to a culture more conducive
to business success. Our objective is a kinder, gentler
culture that produces long-term business success – and 80%
of the employees do some work.

We will expand a bit more on the cultures advocated by the
change meisters; then we will recommend a culture for
success and present some thoughts on how to achieve such
a culture.

What is Corporate Culture

A culture is the way that a group of people usually behave
and the way that they tend to do things. The culture of the
United States is one of freedom to live and work where one
wants, of gadgets and automobiles, of grumbling about the
cost of government, but not participating in improvement,
of limited friendliness and outer garments full of
words/slogans/symbols. Of course the young people have
their subculture, as is the case everywhere in the world.
The current U.S.A. young-person's subculture is
characterized by body piercing, strange drugs, Internet
communications, cell phones, and for young women,
exposing belly buttons.

Corporate culture means the actions and behaviors that the
company forces on its employees by their pay raise system.
Many years ago, the first big corporation that I worked for
had a culture characterized by white shirts and pocket
protectors for production bosses, dress shirts and ties for

technical staff, participation by professionals in community activities and organizations, giving to company-designated charities, never speaking out on problems, professionalism, getting to work ahead of starting time and leaving after quitting time, periodic strikes, union grievances, overpaid production workers and employees who were squeezed to give 110%. My last employer had a kinder and gentler culture, but their kindly culture produced a huge problem that still remains: A significant percentage of the employees do little or no work that contributes to revenues. When I started with the company in the 1960's, I would shake my head and say: How can this company survive with so many people doing next to nothing? At that time, I estimated the percentage to be fifty. By the 1990's, layoffs had reduced this percentage, but I estimate that the percentage was still thirty. I worked in the same department for all of my last thirty-eight years in the factory. The department consisted of about fifteen people in the '60's. It burgeoned to sixty-three in the super seventies and it consisted of eighteen people when I left. If it were my business, I would immediately fire six of those people because they did next to nothing. The company had a big problem. That is why they hired consultants to change our culture. Unfortunately, the culture-change experts only changed the corporate-imposed culture rules and did not solve the company's problem with do-next-to-nothing people. In fact, the do-next-to-nothing people espouse any program that separates them from real work. Here is my exit essay assessment of my company's culture when I left their employ.

Exit Essay: ***The Company Culture – A View from the Factory Floor***

Culture is a relatively new word in industry; so is diversity. I had never heard these words used in the company until about ten years ago. Now we hear these words in almost every management pronouncement. Culture to me means the things that we do all the time and the way that we think most of the time. Culture is what comes automatically to a person in his or her daily life. Each country in the world has a different culture; each ethnic group has a different culture. The company's culture, when I started with the company in the sixties, was one of family, self-confidence, pride, excellence in all activities, keen competition in the marketplace, paternalism (we had many perks) and a touch of nepotism (many families worked at the company). We were the world leader in business; we had the highest market share in most product lines and we were what I call a "winning team." We were number one. I was really proud to say that I worked at the company.

The company's culture changed significantly in the 1980's when we had the first reductions in workforce. Paternalism ended; they took the shoeshine boxes out of the men's room, the bowling alleys were torn up and sold, the softball league was abolished, the foreman's club and superintendent's lunch were shut down. In addition, the "company family" was essentially outlawed. Department social gatherings were discouraged - no more Christmas parties, no more retirement parties, no more 25-year anniversary parties, no more family picnics. We went from being the "company family" to a workforce. The company divorced us.

The next big culture change came with "diversity." "Diversity," as a business word seemed to come to the company with the tenure of a particular CEO. He came onboard when the company was heavily in debt from the purchase of businesses that we knew nothing about. Shortly thereafter "diversity" became the company's mantra. I do not know the company's definition of "diversity," but what it appears to me to mean is that the company gives special treatment and promotions to selected cultures, genders, age groups, ethnic groups and races. Essentially, the company established a rigid policy of discrimination.

Several years ago our department had openings for two engineers. I was assigned to a candidate-screening committee and we were given the instructions that both must meet one or more of the following criteria: be non-Caucasian, be a woman, or have an "alternate lifestyle" (business jargon for a person who advertises his or her sexual proclivities to all). The human resources department (HR) reinforced this edict by only sending us resumes of candidates that met their diversity definition. Essentially, they precluded consideration of mainstream white males.

Another significant culture change came when the "the company values" were imposed on us workers here on the factory floor (managers were exempt). I do not know where the company values came from, but they appear to be something brought in by the CEO who brought in diversity in the mid-nineties. Apparently, somebody must have told the CEO that we were bad employees and that he needed to improve our behavior by giving us a rigid set of behavior guidelines. There are six rules in the company values behavior code. The code is posted multiple times in all departments and conformance to the code is a significant (often the most significant) part of an employee's performance evaluation.

I am sure that the company values were intended to promote employees showing consideration for each other (the golden rule - do unto others as you would have them do unto you) and make the business run better, but many supervisors quickly learned how to use the company values to keep less-favored people from getting raises and even getting rid of employees who may pose a professional threat to him or her. For example, company value #1 is: Respect for individual dignity. Disagreeing with the boss on just about any issue can be a violation of this value. Value #2 is: Uncompromising integrity. Leaving a printer cover sheet at the department printer could result in a violation of this value. Value #3 is trust. Forgetting a meeting with the boss could give a worker a zero in this category for the year. Value #4 is credibility. Spelling a word incorrectly in a report will undoubtedly yield credibility demerits. Value #5 is continuous improvement and renewal. A person could fail this value if he or she did not reduce the number of times that he or she was sick this year compared to last year. Finally, value #6 is recognition and celebration. In my department, you would get a zero in this value if you failed to tell the boss "good meeting" after his monthly department meeting. The extremely disappointing aspect of the company values is that my comments on how supervisors use these values as a weapon are not an exaggeration.

Essentially, the company values changed the company culture to one of mutual distrust and it ended honest communications between employees and coworkers and between employees and management. Employees must scrutinize every spoken and written word to make sure that word would not produce a company value violation. This culture change may best be summarized by a statement that I overheard on the elevator in the building that I work in. When the doors opened, two women were in a heated discussion and I heard one woman say to the other: "The only way to survive at the company is to keep your mouth shut and when they make you talk, only tell them what they want to hear".

The current company culture that is advertised on posters in all buildings is:

"A winning and inclusive culture is:

- *An organization in which all of us freely contribute our ideas and do our best work.*
- *An organization worthy of our talent and participation - a place where people want to work.*
- *A diverse organization that is reflective of our customers and the community."*

As mentioned previously, I feel that the company values precluded open communication of ideas. The dialog and suggestion systems have been abolished and in my department it is financial suicide (no raises) to identify perceived problems. Many company bosses do not accept problems. The second culture claim "the company is a great place to work" certainly runs counter to the feeling that prevails here on the factory floor. Many employees would quit today if their financial and family situation would permit it. Our two new engineers told me that they are just hoping to get five years out of the company. My own son, who I thought would take over for me, quit two weeks ago (after 10 years) to go back to his previous employer. Finally, the company's diversity program makes it impossible to get a promotion or move into management unless you are lucky enough to be a designated "diversity." Essentially, the company practices discrimination in every job consideration. Birth circumstance and sexual proclivity are the most important selection factors.

In summary, I believe that the current company is not what is advertised on the department posters. The real company culture has the following features:

- *There is "silo" behavior at all levels – everybody is afraid to share information lest they become more susceptible to downsizing.*
- *Many employees believe that there is little hope for the future of the company.*
- *There is no enthusiasm for our products.*
- *Managers are clueless; they never go to the factory floor; they have no idea as to who is producing results and who is not, who is considerate, who is not.*
- *The company's focus is on matters other than the business (safety, diversity, reorganization, charity fund raising, etc.).*
- *There is distrust of managers and each other.*
- *There is a complete lack of consideration for each other in most workplaces.*
- *There is no concern for employees as individuals (no company family).*
- *Promotions are based upon birth circumstance or factors other than talent.*
- *There may not be enough talent left to survive.*

Essentially, the company is not a very desirable place to work these days and the current company culture is not very conducive to business success.

What can be done to make the company culture more amenable to business success? The company should scrap the company values behavior code and only ask for mutual consideration and reasonable interpersonal behavior between employees. Stop discrimination in promotion and hiring. Have managers walk the floor daily and learn what their people do and how the business works. Nurture talent. Encourage employees to socialize and get to know their coworkers. And most important of all, focus on the

business at all levels – not on internal projects and societal
programs. The latter is a necessary first step-my opinion.

Wow! I seemed steamed. The Company-Culture program
was probably the worst "foo-foo" plan that I encountered in
my industrial career. When I was working, I used the
adjective "foo-foo" to describe company programs that
were aimed at esoterics: changing behaviors, altering
personalities, dress codes, interpersonal relations, etc. --
programs aimed at changing who we are and how we think.
All of these programs were well intentioned, but when
applied to tens of thousands of people by managers with
only momentary training on the plan usually produced
unintended (and negative) results.

> **RULE:** You cannot change company culture by
> edict or mandatory employee meetings.

Every person is different. People are the way they are
because of their parentage, because of the environment in
which they were reared, because of their current life
situation and environment. I just returned from my first
trip to Portugal and I learned that Moorish influences to the
architecture come from 800 years of occupation by the
Moors. Their intricate details in architecture remain as part
of their culture even though the Moors (whoever they were)
were driven from the country in the twelfth century. Tea
ceremonies are a significant part of the Japanese culture.
One time on a trip to China, a Chinese person made it quite
clear to me that tea ceremonies date back thousands of
years and tea was not introduced into Japan until 1400 A.D.
It probably took a few hundred years, but tea is now a part
of the Japanese culture. Televisions are very much a part
of the culture in many countries. This did not happen
through a consultant's program or through a series of

meetings. My parents did not buy their first TV until I was fourteen years old. Now babies are placed in front of the tube for hours each day and by age two, TV is part of their culture.

> **RULE:** Culture change requires exposure for a significant length of time, usually a lifetime.

My company tried to change its culture to solve the problem of 50% employees doing little or no work and in the year 2000, the culture was as described in my essay and half the people were still not working and the half that worked were angry, as shown by the tone of my essay. I was angry and frustrated.

What is the Ideal Company Culture?

The simple answer to "what is the ideal corporate culture," in my opinion, is one where the employees are qualified for their jobs, happy, well paid, and everybody would like to work there. How does this contrast with the culture advocated by my former employer? Maybe this can best be answered by dissecting the stated culture in my exit essay.

Key statements in company culture statement:

- Freely contribute ideas
- Do our best work
- Worthy of our talent
- Worthy of our participation
- A place where people want to work
- Reflective of our customers
- Reflective of the community

The culture proposed by my company has lots of features that appear to be desirable, but I recognize most features as products of consultant programs. For example, "reflective of our customers and community" means that the racial mix of the company should conform to some established quotas. They had a hiring and layoff program in place to control racial mix. This is certainly not an ideal culture if you are not one of the elect. "Feely contributes ideas" is certainly a desirable component in a company culture, but one would certainly question the honesty of this statement since the company abolished all mechanisms for contributing ideas (the employee dialog system, the suggestion system, product idea system). Maybe they had in mind the Kaisen program that they are trying where employees redesign their department under the guidance of a hired consultant who knows nothing about the business. The other features of company culture seem a bit peculiar. How does an organization become worthy of our talent and participation? The company must meet certain criteria to be worthy of our talent and participation. For example, I would not want to work for a company that did not have good products/or services. This part of the stated culture is probably some kind of psychological strategy that eludes me. It is not straight talk.

RULE: If the person on the street has to ponder the meaning of a company statement, it needs rewriting.

Overall, the culture advocated by my company was an obvious product of consultants and was not a culture, but plan for behavior modification. It was a statement of rules that compliment the company value rules.

Some musts of the ideal company culture are:

- Trust – of each other, of management, of the company
- Integrity – personal, management, company
- Concern – for employees, community, country
- Consideration – employee-to-employee, management-to-employee
- Pay for Contribution – raises go to those who contribute tangible business earnings
- Satisfaction – a feeling that the work you do is necessary and appreciated
- Managers who earned their positions, not who were given positions because of who they know or who they sucked up to
- Free Communications – of ideas, problems, concerns
- Ethics – everything that a company does should meet standards of right and wrong
- Teamwork – employees must share their skills and knowledge and collaborate to make success happen

There may be some attributes that I overlooked, but if you visualize a company with a culture characterized by these ten features, you will have a corporate culture characterized by happy employees. They will be well paid if the company has good products or services that customers want and people will want to work for the company if the word gets out that you have the ideal culture.

RULE: Communicate your corporate culture.

How to Achieve the Ideal Corporate Culture

As mentioned in one of our rules, a culture cannot be dictated or legislated; it develops. Trust develops from consistent honesty in dealing with employees, honesty in dealing with suppliers, honesty in dealing with customers, honesty in dealing with regulatory organizations and governments. I used to have a supervisor who may not have been the best manager (this person was more inclined to get involved with engineering rather than administration), but he was completely honest with us employees and in communicating management directives. He demanded similar honesty from employees. He used to say: "If you cannot trust an employee, you have nothing." If I asked him to loan me $100.00 for three days, he would go into his wallet and hand me the $100.00 (if it was there) with no questions asked. He had complete trust that I would return the money in three days. Similarly, a toddler has complete trust in his or her parents. They learned from birth that parents do things in their best interest. When they are hungry, they feed them; when they get hurt, they comfort them; when they get uncomfortable from soiled diapers, they will change them. They have absolute trust in their parents. The ideal corporate culture has employees who trust managers emphatically, who trust their coworkers not to steal their ideas, not do denigrate them, not to subvert their work, but to assist them in obtaining job success.

> **RULE:** Be honest in all matters and you will obtain the trust of employees, customers, and others.

Corporate integrity, to me, means that the company is proactive in ensuring that all activities are directed in the best interest of the investors as well as being honest. Integrity at the manager level means that managers are really qualified for the jobs that they have. People know their skills and abilities. A person of high integrity will not take an assignment that he or she does not have the appropriate abilities to perform. For example, I would never take on the job of managing investments for an organization because I do not like the stock market and all of my stock market ventures have been less than successful.

Integrity at the employee level similarly means that people not take jobs that they are not qualified to do. If a person is hired to be a toolmaker, he or she should have the machine skills needed for the job. A design engineer should have schooling in engineering fundamentals so that designs do not fail because of lack of knowledge of engineering mechanics or engineering materials. A secretary should know how to type and use pertinent software. A laborer should have the physical abilities to do lifting and the strength aspects of the job. This is one of the biggest failings of my former company. There were many people who were complete frauds. They did not have the education, skills, training, or physical attributes to do the job that they were in. This does a disservice to the corporation and the people themselves will not succeed. Why did this happen? Mostly, this happened because the people were not honest in listing their credentials and managers were not astute enough to discern fact from claim.

> **RULE:** Make every effort to verify that a person is qualified for a job.

Concern for employees is manifested in benefit programs, stock sharing, and other programs that make employees feel a part of the company. The recreation departments that my company used to have were very successful in enkindling a feeling that the company cares about us as individuals. There were after-work clubs on just about every subject, company-owned bowling alleys, a shooting range, tennis courts, ball fields, lunchtime movies -- you name it. One division even had a wooded mountain with a large gathering building at the top. It was used for seminars and parties and the forest was available to employees as a campground. As competition increased, all of these perks were eliminated. A more pragmatic approach would have been to make them self-supporting through user fees. We would have understood.

Concern for the community used to be fostered by company sponsorship of community events, local charity drives, and most beneficial in my community was a summer baseball league that gave thousands of inner city youths a productive and learning way to spend their summer vacation. They also used to offer summer jobs for older youths. On a grand scale, company leaders made substantial contributions to local universities, health organizations, and cultural organizations. Carnegie Hall was built by an industry leader concerned for his community. Charles Mott, one of the founders of General Motors, kept the city of Flint, Michigan alive throughout his life and his foundation is still saving the city from ruin. This is company concern for the community. It does not have to be grand and expensive, but all companies should have a strategy to show concern for the community.

Concern for the country can be manifested by paying for military leaves, by promoting participation in election to government office. Even part-time mayor jobs and the like require company help such as time off for must-attend meetings. When times got rough, the company fired a number of state legislators. A proper company strategy will find a way to accommodate elected officeholders. They could be part of the company's government relations' function. As it stands now, in U.S. industry, hardly any "employees" run for elected office. Their employers make it too rough. This is wrong and the democracies of the world will become closed cells open only to the wealthy and to entrepreneurs who use running for office as subsidized advertising for their business.

RULE: Show that you care as a company.

Consideration among employees means that you treat coworkers as if you would like to be treated and you do not do anything that annoys the people around you. For example, when I left my company, employee-to-employee consideration had decayed to the point where every person could have a boom box on his or her desk playing loud enough to be heard within a hundred yard radius. Needless-to-say, when there are twenty people in adjoining cubicles, each with a radio, there is a cacophony that absolutely precludes intelligent thought. I used to seek out empty conference rooms to do work. Production areas had hard rock playing over loudspeakers at about a 110 dB level. You had to shout to communicate. I have no idea how this lack of consideration for others (those who do not like hard rock or gospel) proliferated throughout the company, but it sure showed in product quality. People cannot do good work when they are irritated all day by music that they cannot stand.

All radios and personal address systems playing music should be banned in every company. If a person has a mindless, monotonous job that could be made easier by music, we have the technology to let this happen while respecting the space of others. I wear a radio headset jogging and riding my bike and it disturbs no one else. Every manager should make a concerted effort to ensure that no employee in his or her charge does anything that shows a lack of consideration for others, no blaring radios, no loud talking, no off-color jokes, no gambling, no preaching, no offensive smells, and no offensive mannerisms.

> **RULE:** Have everyone respect the workspace of others.

Companies show consideration for employees by making them part of what is happening, by not treating them as chattel, by not talking down to us, by making us feel like we are a part of the company. If you are a manager, do not use the term "my people." We are not your serfs. We are employees. We can understand letters written by top management. You do not have to call a department meeting and re-read the letter. We are not idiots. We do not like to be surprised by announcements that our division is being dissolved and we have five working days to network another job in the company. Major changes do not happen instantly, we like to be apprised of changes that may be necessary and we need time to adjust our lives.

> **RULE:** Show consideration for employees in all statements and changes. Give them warning when warning is due.

Employees deserve fair pay. It is fair to pay big bosses lots of money because they have more responsibility and usually have no free time? Their life is their work. I will never forget when I was an engineering student one of my fellow students did a calculation on what it cost the company for its CEO to go to the bathroom. As you may expect, a significant savings could be realized if the CEO soiled his or her cloths and the company replaced them daily. Corporate executives probably make too much money, but they deserve higher salaries than workers with less responsibility and from whom less is required. Some executives abuse their positions for personal gain. This of course, is unethical and a strategy should be in place to prevent it.

As an example, in my early years as a materials engineer, I was consulted on a wide variety of problems. One that was referred to me by our construction division turned out to be associated with installing a swimming pool in a company vice-president's backyard. Executive abuse of position was rampant. Things were better when I left the company, but the rumor on the factory floor was that a departing CEO negotiated life use of the corporate jet as a farewell gift.

> **RULE:** Take steps to prevent executive abuse of position.

On the other end of the spectrum, an ideal corporate culture has a pay for results/performance system that satisfied even the lowest paid workers. They need to feel that their pay is just and there needs to be counseling to convince production workers that running a computer-controlled bottling machine is not a job worth $20.00 per hour; it should pay a "living wage" as defined by some U.S. government organizations. Of course, all raises should be based upon increased contribution to earnings – nothing else.

> **RULE:** Pay your lowest-paid employees a living wage that reflects the local labor market.

Every employee survey that I have ever seen shows job satisfaction as the number one factor in producing happy employees. There is nothing worse in this world than a boring job. Even lazy people abhor such a job. An ideal company culture includes a methodology for assessing the satisfaction that workers derive from their daily tasks and continually address ways to improve job satisfaction. The simplest and often most effective approach is to make sure that each worker knows how their job contributes to company earnings. If an assembly line worker spends his day putting a screw in a hole, take the time to show that person the entire manufacturing operation. Let that person see how he or she is a vital link, an essential part of the team.

> **RULE:** Work to make all employees feel that their work contribution is an essential part of the business.

We spent a whole chapter on the need for qualified managers and another on qualified employees. The ideal corporate culture abhors suck-ups, and people are promoted on ability to produce increased earnings or business results. There is nothing as destructive in a company or organization as the practice of giving promotions to those who have not earned them.

> **RULE:** Promotions must be earned.

I have a pet peeve about "free communications" in a company. I have always been a strong supporter of getting the opinion of others on every project that I propose. Without fail, the project results were improved by suggestions from others. This holds true in all matters:

personal, work, community. I was devastated when my company eliminated their suggestion system. I was doubly devastated when they eliminated the "dialog" system that I used frequently. They had forms in racks everywhere in the corporation and an employee could anonymously write up a concern and a coordinator would see that the concern got a timely response from an appropriate manager. Near the end, this program only cost the company one person's salary. There was only one coordinator for the corporation. This was still too high a cost. The program was scrapped. I presented a modified plan to the CEO that would cost nothing for coordination, but they were no longer interested in upward communication in any form. How disappointing; how destructive; how costly.

> **RULE:** Encourage employee input in all
> matters at all levels.

Corporate ethics is what I am advocating through this book. This book is an act of desperation. The dishonesty, the impropriety, the deceit, the greed, the lack of consideration, the hostility, the illegality, the environmental disregard that I have witnessed over my forty-three years on the factory floor forced me to write this book. As I write this sentence, I full well realize that this piece of yellow legal paper may end up in the garbage with many others and this book may never be published. In fact, I suspect that the odds are 80/20 against publication, but I must try. Things are so wrong in U.S. industry; things are so wrong in U.S. government organizations. There is little ethics. Ethics is what is right and what is wrong. Sure there are opinions on right and wrong, but we all know fundamental wrongs. We all know that it is not in the interest of civilized society to kill another; it is not right to steal your neighbor's possessions; it is not right to be mean and nasty to your neighbor; it is not right to ignore rules implemented to create order in our society. People know what is ethical and people know what is right and wrong in running an organization.

RULE: Make ethics in all matters corporate priority.

Teamwork is the outcome of effective communications. It is getting input from others and enlisting their help to achieve a common goal. I have managed many building projects outside of work. For the past twenty-five years, we have had at least four houses that we rent and, of course, the only way to survive financially is to do all the maintenance and construction work yourself. We have always bought "distressed" houses because of budget constraints, so each house that we put on line needed "gutting." We enlist the help of family members for these projects and this is where I have witnessed teamwork the way it was meant to be. I post the jobs that have to be done and the team members pick one that appeals to them and do it. They work at their own pace and do the job using the tools and methods that they prefer. They are empowered to get the job done in their way. When one task is done, each person takes another. We have a celebration when the job is done, but they are not paid. They work as a team to get the house ready for market. That is the goal. Job satisfaction comes from knocking off tasks on the to-do list.

We were so successful because we had key elements of teamwork: an achievable goal, empowered workers, complete trust (they are my wife, kids and in-laws and my father), they were nice to each other (they are family), they were doing the job because they wanted to, and they knew that they would be rewarded by a nice dinner at the end and a few pleasant lunches at the completion of milestones. There is no way that my wife and I could complete major house renovations without our team. Teamwork makes things happen, but it requires the right kind of environment. Sports teams work because all members are motivated to win. Military teams (company, battalion, squad, etc.) work because all team members want to best the enemy. Many company teams do not work because they lack direction (the punch list) and they often have members who subvert each other's work. Internal friction prevents success. Trust may be lacking.

> **RULE:** Teamwork is essential for business results. Make teams happen.

Overall, the ideal corporate culture is based upon ethics, good products, and a favorable work environment; that is, an environment characterized by satisfying work, just pay, consideration for each other, and leaders of the highest integrity. A company cannot legislate a culture change as mine tried to do. You must earn an ideal culture.

CHAPTER 9:   Company Programs

What Programs?

In my early days in industry "company programs" were
suggestions from management to participate in certain
activities that the company espoused. For example, in my
first engineering job, my employer, a very large
corporation, encouraged professionals at my plant to join
the local Chamber of Commerce. They paid our
membership dues. They also had a variety of programs to
make us buy company products. We got significant
discounts and family members also got discounts. They
were quite benign programs and some were really
employee benefits. My last employer always had a huge
company program aimed at making employees donate a
significant amount of money to a particular charity. It was
really not optional. I witnessed a person fired because he
did not give one year. The church that he belonged to had a
very destructive fire and he donated more than ten percent
of his salary to his church that year. Of course, the
company denied that his firing had anything to do with not
giving to the designated charity, but all of us on the factory
floor knew that it was. I used to play bridge at lunch with a
group of managers and one day, one boasted that he based
raises on how much an employee gave to the designated
charity. He did not know that most employees were wise to
his scheme and they took appropriate action. If he made a
person give an extra hundred dollars that year, he or she did
not complain or argue, he or she just cheerfully signed the
pledge card, and sometime during the year took home a
hundred dollars worth of company equipment or supplies.
This occurred in a skilled trades department where one drill
bit could be worth $100.00 and most participated in this
"employee payback" program.

The point of this story is that programs that force something on employees often do not do what they were intended to do. When business got more competitive, my last employer barraged us with one program after another. Most were concocted by outside consultants; some were more cult than program; some were just plain worthless; some were too shallow; some too "hairy." Some programs were excellent and the company got their money's worth. Unfortunately, at this point in time, I can only think of one program, elementary statistics for everyone that, fit the excellent category. However, the problem that we are addressing in this chapter is that most company programs at my last employer contained useful nuggets that could help the business, but all, except for forced donation to the company charity, were fleeting. The company did not carry through and implement the "useful nuggets" from these programs in the long term. A second problem with my company's programs is that when company improvement/behavior modification programs are purchased from consultants, they come across to us workers on the factory floor as insincere. They are just another hula-hoop fad. In talking with my colleagues in the technical community, I believe that consultant-generated programs are rampant and many of my colleagues were victims of the same programs that I was subjected to. The consultants are also effective marketers.

The purpose of this chapter is to present my reaction to some of the major company programs that were administered to me at my last employer. The objective of doing so is to advocate that large companies and organizations think seriously about buying from the outside, and they should only institute programs that can be continued and become part of company culture. For example, every business/organization or government should have continuous improvement as part of their culture and as the employees participate in creation of the program they are more likely to believe and follow what is preached. Homemade is usually better than processed.

The format of this chapter is the same as the other chapters. My exit essay will be presented and we will describe some of the more memorable programs and why they met or missed the mark and we will conclude with some suggestions for programs that can continually improve business.

Memorable Programs

I have been the victim of so many corporate programs that it is difficult to decide where to start in recalling the fun and enjoyment. At one time, my company had a huge building just to house the staff that they maintained to teach in-house "courses." The "courses" were almost all some type of concocted program, not fundamentals like mathematics, chemistry, writing, etc. In 1995 or thereabouts, our newly acquired CEO mandated that all company employees take forty hours of training per year as a job requirement. Each manager was tracked to see if he or she had 100% compliance. Needless-to-say, we were forced to get our forty hours in. Failure to do so meant no raise and number one on the layoff list. I was very much in favor of the program since I typically attended at least three technical conferences each year that would count toward my forty hours. One conference was always a week long so I would get my forty hours in easily. The down side was that the company stopped paying for my travel cost and registration fees for conferences in 1997, it typically cost me $10,000 of my money and ten days of my vacation to attend the conferences that were necessary for me to keep up in my technical field.

Many of my coworkers here on the factory floor took the company "courses" that were mostly useless. The machinist who was part of my technical team was sent to a computer school to fulfill his forty-hour requirement. He did not have access to a computer in his shop or at home. The company was big on lunchtime courses. I forget to mention that in my department we had to find a way to get our forty hours of training on our own time. I took vacation for any training; most of my coworkers had to spend their lunch hours going to bogus in-house courses. I went to a series of software introductions taught by one of the company "networks" (these networks were essentially minority/diversity clubs). The instructors were sincere and well intentioned, but they did not know enough about the subject to teach it. They really stumbled and I learned next to nothing.

Before I go on to describe more company programs, here is my exit essay that covers some of the more memorable ones.

Exit Essay: *Company Programs - A View from the Factory Floor*

Last Friday I had lunch in a restaurant and a woman at a nearby table was wearing a T-shirt emblazoned with "Making Strides Against Best practices." She was wearing a company pass around her neck; she was obviously a company employee. After lunch I stopped at the employee store to pick up some items. The woman in front of me in the checkout line spent $106.43 on gift items and charged them to her department. These women undoubtedly were participating in one of the company's consultant programs. Here on the factory floor we have been besieged with these programs for the past twenty years or so. Sometimes we have three or four concurrent *programs to deal with. Most of these programs are concocted by business consultants and sold to the company at significant cost. There is a rumor here on the floor that the company paid the one consulting company 42 million dollars for a program to be used at just one division. In addition, I estimate that it cost another 20 million dollars to send 10,000 of us to their 8-hour introductory course.*

Are these programs worth the cost? Do they increase sales, quality, profits, work life quality? Most of these programs contain at least one kernel (I got that word from one of the programs) of mutual benefit, but the company invariably allows these programs to die before they produce any measurable value. Somebody in upper management meets another consultant and we move on to the next program. Next year at this time, the employees that I saw last Friday will undoubtedly be involved with some new programs. The company needs to establish improvement programs that are sustainable and produce business results. The remainder of this essay will present my reactions to some memorable programs that I participated in and I will conclude with my suggestions for a sustainable program.

Adviser – This is the biggest program (in cost and participation) that I have participated in and it was probably the one that produced the least positive results. Just last week it netted us a new rash of racial discrimination lawsuits. It is the belief here on the factory floor that this program was initiated as a response to previous racial discrimination lawsuits. The consultants who developed the program probably sold it to as a way to prevent all discrimination lawsuits. This program was supposed to convert the workforce into one big loving family. The program selected hundreds of candidates, and each received 180 hours of social-behavior indoctrination over a several-month period. Trained "Advisers" are supposed to become role models of the desired employee behavior.

The most common reaction to the Adviser program here on the factory floor is that the company created hundreds of department "snitches" who are supposed to warn management of potential behavior/discrimination problems. In addition, the Advisers were encouraged by their trainers to "spill their guts" in the training classes and the consultants recorded the problems that were brought to light. Some of the employee concerns identified in one Adviser group were:

- *Downsizing fears control most employee actions*
- *There is widespread lack of trust*
- *Employees do not feel good about the company's future*
- *Funding is not available*
- *The company is not investing in the future*
- *Each company building is like a separate kingdom*
- *Plans for the future are well kept secrets*
- *No communications*
- *Employee energy is low*
- *No new products*
- *The company is a prison environment*
- *Managers command and control; they do not lead.*
- *Employees are viewed as overhead not assets*

Most of the issues identified were real, however, little is being done to address them. Use of Advisers as a force to correct negative behaviors is fizzling because they have no defined duties or action items. If I were asked to spend 42 million dollars on an employee betterment program, I would have asked the consultants to produce demonstrated results in another comparable size company before signing on the dotted line. Discrimination is rampant at the company, especially age discrimination, and I have never seen a more hostile work environment (my own) in my 43 years in industry.

Department Operating System (DOS) - To me, this program is industrial engineering rediscovered and lathered with Japanese foo-foo. What appears to be new is using machine operators to act as part of a methods study. Of course, this part of DOS is a good idea. What looks like a bad idea to me is that the consultants who sold this program to the company do not want engineers involved. They say that if a machine needs redesign, the operators will do it. I know of an instance where the DOS team moved production machines around to reduce the number of steps that an operator takes, but they introduced a new product defect in the process. They moved huge machines from near the building walls to the center of floor spans. Now the floor deflects from machine motion and this deflection changes tool relationships and a product defect is now present where we had none. Nobody on the DOS team knew enough about engineering to calculate floor deflections and nobody knew about vibration analysis of machines. On its present course, this program may destroy a number of product lines before it is put out of its misery. I suggest the return of an industrial engineering function in the company's reorganized engineering division (my plan is coming). The company should use science, engineering and operator involvement sans foo-foo.

TP – This program spread through various company divisions over the past year or two. Fortunately, it is relatively dormant now, but it did very substantial damage wherever it was fully implemented. In this program, a clueless department supervisor walks around his or her department and makes employees throw out all machines and materials that are not in use at this instant in time. It is cleanup insanity. Last week an engineer came to us with a frantic request for help in solving a problem with a particular product. Japanese customers are refusing to accept this product because it is packaged poorly compared with the competition. We had the piece of equipment in our lab that could be used to solve this problem, but it was TPed about six months ago. It was the corporation's only device that could quantify package integrity. It was a laser triangulation device built at a cost of about $300,000 and I used it on problems about once a year. I fought for two years to keep the TP-people from throwing out this machine, but they got it earlier this year when I was away on business.

I suspect that one of our competitors paid a consultant to develop this program and sell it to the company. Who would throw out their snow blower each summer because it would not be used till next winter? Who would throw out a diamond ring because it is only worn once in three years? Who would throw out a plumber's helper because it has not been used in five years? There are tools that are seldom used, but when you need them you need them. If an employee feels that he or she needs a particular piece of equipment to do their job, their decision should be respected. The TP program never saved a penny as far as I can see, but it has inflicted severe damage to the Corporation's competitive capability.

Manage by data (MBD) – This program was a bit simplistic, but it was a valiant attempt to get company managers to make data-based decisions. A new quality control director brought it to the company. Unfortunately, he only stayed a brief time. I liked the concept of having a department's production problems summarized on a single sheet of paper along with action items and people responsible for addressing the problems. Many of the MBD examples that I was a part of used rather "fuzzy" data, but the MBD probably would have yielded some company value if it was sustained. I think that it is now deceased – another dropped opportunity. The champion left and most managers lost interest.

CSEDD – I have no idea what this acronym stood for, but this was a huge program to make us somewhat literate in basic statistics. Everyone at the company had to take the basic 16-hour course. Management was on a statistics kick at the time and they would give us directives in statistics jargon. For example, we were told that we had to all work toward a CpK of less than 2 or some such thing. This was another good program allowed to whither on the vine. By the time that we were trained, management was off on another program. My department, at least, retained the use of statistical tests of differences in our lab studies. There are probably other limited examples where this program produced an enduring effect, but not many.

Six alpha – This was a program that came with a new CEO. We all got trained in the meaning of six alpha and how it would make us the most profitable company in the world. Six alpha means only one part in a million will fail in use. People tried to implement it in selected places, but I have yet to witness a company manufacturing operation that is within this failure rate on components or final products.

Risk Analysis - This program died about ten years ago. It was another attempt to improve the decisions made by company managers. The consultant who sold the company this program applied probability mathematics to the factors that go into the decision-making process. They developed a *model that allowed a number to be placed on business alternatives. If the number to build a plant was 8, and the number to not build was 4, you build. This program had a lot of value in that it forced managers to consider all pertinent factors before making important decisions. It died probably because the math got a bit complicated, but the company should have at least retained the concept of making managers consider data and facts before making business decisions.*

Albert Smith – This program was called some acronym that I do not remember, but essentially the company hired Dr. Albert Smith to show us how to improve the corporation. Dr. Smith was a clinical psychologist who spent most of his career as a resident psychologist at a number of metal-health institutions. He came up with a system for improving the behavior of mental patients and hypothesized that his system would also work in industry. Essentially, he advocated recording incremental improvements in behavior and instantly rewarding positive improvements and punishing negative behaviors. Here on the factory floor, we were told to pick out the worst problem that we had in our department, quantify it, develop an improvement program, and graph our progress in improving the problem. Documented improvements were rewarded with gold stamps that we could put on our foreheads. We graphed just about everything, had lots of meetings, and the best part, many meetings had donuts.

Of course it died, but who can argue that continuous improvement is necessary. We need to go back to Dr. Smith's concept of always having continuous improvement programs, but leave out the hoopla and donuts. Do it because it is the right thing to do in a winning company.

Others – There are many other programs that we have been victims of, but this essay is already too long so I will just mention some active and defunct programs with a comment on their status and value:

- *Teamwork – good concept, but barely alive because silos reign*
- *Black shirt – this is statistics with more Japanese foo-foo; it is not doing well – too much foo-foo I think*
- *Designer clothing as rewards – the company spent a fortune on t-shirts and jackets, but they only irritated those who did not get clothed*
- *Benchmarking peer companies – this program is still warm, but there is no evidence that it produces business results*
- *Experiment Improvement (statistical design) – this program is selectively practiced and I suspect that the concept is flawed; it is too complicated to produce action items*
- *Safety as job one – this is the company's most important program, much more important than business success*
- *Record retention – this program is only warm; most files are back to being messy*
- *Process control – this program never really happened; it should have*
- *Company charity – this is the company's most vibrant and enduring program (because your job and raises depend on how much you give)*

In summary, here on the factory floor, we have been subjected to too many programs with a variety of objectives, but overall they were invented to improve our work life and company profits. Most programs died because they were too denigrating or complicated to survive. These programs were developed by outside consultants and force-fit to our business. Often times the fit was not right. Employees played no role in the design of these programs. If it were my company, I think that I would develop a program aimed at ethical behavior, neat appearance, neat workplace, congenial behavior, continuing education, knowledge of statistics and continuous improvement as conditions of employment. In addition, I would insist that managers learn their businesses and give timely "thank you's" (not shirts or jackets) for exemplary results. I think that such a system may last – my opinion.

I hope that my exit essay presented the flavor of what I mean about company programs. There were lots and most died after a brief life. They were attempts to improve the business, but most only irritated the employee victims. Failure of these programs can probably be attributed to insincerity. Managers were not on board at any level. I suspect that the human resources department concocted some and others came from consultant ads in manager journals or some such place. There were no employee surveys to see if these programs would meet needs or produce some business result. I conclude this section with a mention of two programs that will forever be in my mind. One was an eight-hour motivational talk by several world-renowned "business improvers." There were at least four speakers and all wrote several books on how to run companies. They were great speakers; one was hilarious. He did a ten-minute comedy routine about the little bottles of shampoo and other stuff that they have in better hotel bathrooms. After eight hours of getting pumped up by the best business consultants in the company, I walked away with one nugget.

"Always stay at a Ritz Carlton if you want freedom from pretzel crumbs in the carpeting."

The other program that I fondly remember from my last employer was employee stock options. Company management decided that we employees would work better if we were all stockholders. We would have a financial stake in the success of the company. They instituted a program with great fanfare to give each of us an option to buy 100 shares of the company stock at $55.00. It was $70.00 when they made the announcement. By the time that we got the paperwork, the stock was down to $40.00. I am writing this two years after we got our stock options and the stock has never even seen $30.00 in the past two years. Now I understand that they are "restructuring" the program to find a way to get stock options that are less, not more, than the selling price of the stock. Another program that missed the mark.

A Continuous Improvement Program

After all these years and all these programs, I am of the opinion that the only program that companies or organizations need is continuous improvement in all important matters. I really liked the basic concept of the Albert Smith program where departments, teams, and any group charged with a task meet once or twice a year and identify a business matter that needs improvement. It could be a process, procedure, machine, marketing function, advertising, collaboration, an environmental issue, and even interpersonal relations – anything that is costing more money than it should or that is in some way having a negative effect on business results. For the executive committee, it might be market share. Identify the improvement project, institute a plan to make things better and then track progress. Celebrate success. If you fail, regroup and take another approach. It does not have to be a formal or fancy program. A simple graph of department scrap in units/month may be the only metric needed. When you complete a project, start another. Participation and enthusiasm in improvement programs could be part of every employee's performance appraisal.

In addition to programs in every work group, individuals should have a similar improvement program for themselves. Ask yourself what can I do or learn that would make me more valuable to the company and contribute to business success. Would it help to learn Powerpoint? Would it help me and the company if I took a stress analysis course at a university? Would it help me and the company if I went to night school and obtained a master's degree in business administration? I firmly believe that it is an employee's responsibility to pay for these types of personal improvement initiatives.

> **RULE:** Personal continuous improvement programs are the individual's responsibility.

Needless-to-say, if a company wants to be magnanimous and pay for tuition and cost for personal improvement projects, then take the money; but every working person has the responsibility to buy his or her "tools." Everyone expects a tradesperson like a plumber, electrician, carpenter, landscaper, painter, etc. to bring their own tools. If you are a skilled tradesperson in a big company, you need to buy your own tools as well. The exception to the rule is computers and software in big companies. I lived through the introduction of the personal computer in industry. It was chaos at the start. Every department had different equipment and software and none would "talk to each other." There were "Apple people," "IBM people," "Shack people," and other clans. It was terrible.

> **RULE:** A company needs to have a computer strategy (that makes business sense).

Getting back to the issue of employees paying for their improvement plans themselves, there is nothing but bickering if the company or organization selectively supports individual initiatives. You cannot win. If the company sends a person to a computer school, other employees will come forward with their school proposals. Managers then have to explain how the company will benefit more from Joe going to "Labwear School" than from Mary going to a FEM course at the local university. Raises can reflect appropriate remuneration for personal improvement programs.

In summary, I have been through many company programs that were supposed to increase productivity, save cost, increase sales, and make us like each other and many programs to teach new skills and ways of doing things. None of the consultant-contrived programs lasted more than a few years and the good aspects of these programs soon disappeared.

Instead, I advocate continual improvement projects that address current problems and solve them. These will never stop; they should be part of company culture. Personal improvement programs should also continue throughout your life. You never know enough. You never have all the skills that your intellect can absorb. There is always more space on your disk.

Chapter 10:   Human Resources/Relations

Problem

The Cartoon, "Dilbert,"[®] depicts an evil cat, "Catbert," as the human resource/relations (HR) person in Dilbert's fictitious company. I do not often have the opportunity to read the "funnies" in the newspaper, but the last time that I did a Dilbert coworker announced that he was leaving the company and he asked Catbert how he can meet his pre-employment agreement that says that he will not take away any skills or knowledge obtained on the job. "How can I forget what I know?" he asked. The next frame shows Catbert attaching a suction machine to the engineer's head. The last frame shows the guy walking away with a head the size of a golf ball. Catbert yells, "Better stay away from golf courses." Dilbert creates the image that HR people are vicious enemies of employees. The problem addressed in this chapter is that in my opinion, the HR department in my company mutated into a Catbert times ten, and I suspect the departments at other U.S. companies have Catberts.

In the old days, we had a personnel department, which took care of training education programs, new hires, layoffs, leaves, benefits and leaving the company. In many companies at that time (1960's), the personnel department also administered the company suggestion system. In fact, in my co-op years, I spent four months as a suggestions investigator, and as a co-op student, I worked for the training director. It was a healthy, happy department that provided significant service to production and support departments. It was about ten people for a total employment of three thousand. I thought that they did a great job. There was a union at this company, but the labor relations department (3 people), handled these negotiations. We had strikes every time that the union contract was renewed, but there was order and union employees were back to normal as soon as the union leaders told them that everything was okay.

How did "Human Resources" happen to American industry? I do not know, but it sure took the order and civility out of my company's personnel department. I think that the mutation started in the 1980's. That is when tough times and global competition started. My company's HR department started the programs that we discussed in the previous chapter. They became an adversary of employees and a weapon for managers. They acquired some of the meanest women that I have ever encountered and I believe that they depleted the company's technical talent by offering retirement programs that could not be refused. To exacerbate the technical talent problem, they took over all decision-making on new hires and provided only diversity candidates, not candidates that may have needed skills. In other words, my company's HR department went from a personnel department that provided services to employees and managers to a liability that damaged the company to its core. I suspect HR departments throughout U.S. industry come from the same mold.

It is the purpose of this chapter to present the reasons why I grew to hate my last HR department with the hope that recounting my tribulations will point the way to a company restructuring that will remove the potentially destructive power from other HR departments. We will present my exit essay and make a proposal on how to modernize administrative personnel and benefits administration. We hope to convince corporate executives that HR as it presently exists should perish from the earth. (Forgive the angry tone; just the use of "H's" and "R's" in the same sentence sets me off.)

The HR Dilemma

What happened to personnel departments? Consultants, I suspect. "Personnel" has a dictionary definition: "A body of people employed in any occupation," was the definition given in my company-issue desktop dictionary. There was no definition for human resources in my dictionary, but maybe the term is a take-off from "natural resources." I suppose that the name change reflects a change from providing services to employees to an organization that dispenses people as needed by business units. They have become a purveyor of people without employee services. And that is a shame. Social order dictates rules, standards, and somebody to enforce them. Personnel departments used to establish rules of behavior and if there were people who were disrupting social order, they served as the advocate for those offended by people who display aberrant behavior, for abusive managers, for discrimination, for incompetence. The HR department at my last employer had no part of employee advocacy. If there was racial discrimination in a department, a lawsuit was the only option; if there was stealing, we were taught to look the other way; if certain workers were abusive to others, we were forced to endure this abuse in silence.

> **RULE:** Corporations and large organizations
> need social order.

My exit essay cites a personal example of frustration over a wrong behavior and other HR problems. Hopefully, it provides a window into what happens when an HR department becomes the adversary of employees.

Exit Essay: *Human Resources Activities – A View from the Factory Floor*

For thirty-five of my thirty-eight years with the Company I had no dealings with the Human Resources (HR), department. There have always been a significant number of HR employees in the building that I worked in, and as far as I knew, the only thing that they did was process the paper work for new hires, layoffs and retirees. Occasionally, they conducted information sessions to explain a new benefit reduction. To me, they were a benign department. All big companies seem to have an HR department and managers seem to accept them as a necessary part of doing business. HR departments are a tradition in American industry.

However, in the last three or four years, to my dismay, I learned that the company's seemingly benign HR department is mostly evil, an incontrovertible adversary of company employees, the sponsor of meaningless surveys, and their involvement in hiring of technical staff has dealt a significant blow to the Company's technical talent base. If the company is to survive, its HR department must be significantly changed. The following explains how and why I grew to feel that the company's HR is something that must be fixed.

The adversarial nature of the company's HR department - *The Company was a successful company for much of my career. The division where I worked was fat, dumb and happy; there were probably three support staff for every production worker and there were twice as many production workers than needed. Division employment was as high as 30,000 people in the 1970's (there were about 60 people in my department) and I would sometimes look around my department and muse: "We could do what we* *do with one third the employees that we have." Now we are one-third the size that we were (20 people), and we still have people in the department that do next to nothing.*

About three years ago, one of our do-nothing (my opinion) male employees decided to put the rush on a woman employee that I relied on to do work for me. I observed that they were having long chat sessions; then I saw them going to the cafeteria for bagels in the morning and coffee in the afternoon; then they progressed to leaving for a workout in the company gym from 11:30 to about 1:15. They would then eat lunch and then go for coffee. The work output of the employee that I used to rely on dropped to nil and what she did do for me became careless, sloppy, and of questionable value.

I went to the boss and asked him to do something about this situation. He told me that he would look into the matter. About a month later nothing improved and I asked him if he looked into this matter. He told me that he talked with the individuals and they assured him that they were not doing anything inappropriate, "they are just friends," and that I should drop the matter. Eventually, I tried to resolve the matter through HR. This is when I discovered that if you try to right what you perceive to be a wrong behavior, you would become victim of the full wrath of the HR department as well as most of company management. To blow the whistle on a perceived wrong is career suicide – worse than whistle blowing in the federal government. I will skip the details here, but I carried this issue as far as the corporate head of HR to no avail. The department relationship that cost the company a lot of money eventually cooled off, but I forever lost trust in the work of these individuals.

So this is the primary reason for my negative impression of the HR department and why I feel that they are the adversaries of all company employees. Unfortunately, I later learned that my encounter was not an isolated HR reaction. The machinist who does work for our lab, told me that he once reported that several of his coworkers were taking afternoons off and charging the time to jobs. He lost his raise for the year for bringing this to his supervisor's attention and nothing was done to the employees who were skipping out on work. Some company "Advisers," who are also company supervisors, told the program organizers that they would essentially lose their jobs if they reported discrimination or other behavior problems in their departments to their supervisors or to HR. I suspect that the root cause of the uselessness of the company's HR department in the area of people problems is that business units essentially fund HR and the business units do not want to hear about people problems. They keep business unit support as long as they suppress people issues.

HR Hiring practices - I mentioned in a previous essay that the company's HR department is currently enforcing a discrimination policy that requires at least 70 percent of new hires to be from their list of selective diversity people. Their definition of diversity seems to be: African American, Hispanic, female, homosexual, lesbian, trans-sexual, Asian, or Native American. White males are excluded from employment consideration. The company's HR people also select professionals only from selected universities. Apparently, they are reflecting the allegiances of HR managers and business unit managers. They do not select candidates on talent, but rather see to it that incoming employees meet their discrimination agenda.

Surveys and assessments – Another HR function that should be changed in a big way is the surveys that they *conduct to obtain employee feedback and the surveys that they allegedly do to assess the competency of supervisors. HR hires an outside agency for the annual employee satisfaction survey, but the HR administrators usually allow only questions that are not relevant and HR (or management) never does anything with the survey data. Here on the factory floor, we are shown the results summarized to look as good as possible, and there are never any action items to address even the most significant employee concerns.*

This year HR conducted an assessment of managers at my company division. I do not know what questions they asked in the survey or who they asked, but the managers that we workers considered to be complete clowns and destructive to the business were assessed as "OK" and other supervisors that I know to be very intelligent and conscientious got poor ratings. It appears that they assessed social skills, clothing choice, and sports prowess rather than leadership skills and business knowledge. Again, I give the company's HR department a failing rating. These surveys should be drafted and conducted by professionals with demonstrated results in improving people/manager relationships in our type of industry.

Overall, I am of the opinion that the company would be much better off as a corporation if the HR department was dissolved and replaced with a benefits/employee relations department. The benefits part of the department would handle benefit programs as well as paper work for new hires, layoffs and retirements. People problems would be the responsibility of the employee relation's part of the department. People problems would be mediated. A mediation team could consist of a corporate mediator, a department mediator, and the department supervisor. Department mediator could be a rotating position assigned to various trusted employees. There could be a corporate mediator council to develop company behavior guidelines/policies, but the current HR adversary system is doing nothing but creating employee hostility. They have no knowledge of department situations; they do not have psychological training (by my observation) and they do not have the people skills needed (by my observation). In my opinion, they are mostly "nasty people" (based upon my treatment).

Recruiting of talent can be accomplished through contract with one of the many employment agencies that are available worldwide. These organizations can identify candidate talent for any position without the discrimination and biases of the company's HR department. The outside firm should have a directive to hire the best person disregarding all factors but academic credentials, previous work results, and documentation that the candidate has the skills that the position requires.

Essentially, I am suggesting that the company would be in a much better position for recovery if its Human Resources Department was dissolved and replaced by outside professionals on an as-needed basis. My personal experiences with the company's HR department over the past few years have shown me that this organization is certainly not adding value and that our customers certainly would not pay for what they do – my opinion.

I was particularly disturbed when I learned the HR department just did not want to hear about an employee problem, much less do anything about it. It is none of my business what people do away from work, but when a person who is supposed to be doing technician work for me stops doing my work, I am affected. I wanted the problem solved.

> **RULE:** An HR department should be the advocate
> for personnel issues.

My company's HR department's hiring practices were the antithesis of ethics. They knowingly were putting people into jobs knowing full well that they were not qualified to do the job. The plant where I worked, in fact, hired an HR director who was hired because he was a "minority." His background was in HR in a hotel chain. As HR Manager for the plant where I worked, he was calling the shots on hiring engineers and scientists to keep the business going. Was he qualified to do this? I think not. The word on the factory floor was that he was hired to re-staff the plant with minorities. He was director of discrimination.

> **RULE:** Hiring should be non-discriminatory.

The other big failing of my company's HR department was that they were supposed to survey employees, sense their mood, and find out where people problems exist, where people are dissatisfied, where there is an incompetent boss. The surveys that they conducted were a convoluted mess that yielded no useable data – mostly because of obtuse questions. Here is an example from one of these employee surveys:

- My accomplishments are recognized in a way that is meaningful to me.
- I believe that the company's business plans will ensure our long-term success.
- Management demonstrates that employees are important to company success.

- My employee development plan builds skills to help me remain competitive in the future.

Answer one:

[ ] Strongly disagree [ ] Disagree [ ] Neither agree or disagree [ ] Agree [ ] Strongly agree

They never seem to use straight talk. How about:

Does the boss thank you when you show special effort?

Do you understand the company's business plan?

Do managers talk to employees as equals?

Is the company helping you to build your skills?

5 is "yes" -- 1 is "no"

Their questions smack with insincerity and doublespeak. They are unquestionably purchased material, which further shows that HR is aloof of employees. They do not make up questions that might show management in a bad light. HR exists at the behest of management and they know that suppressing employee unrest or dissatisfaction will help them keep their jobs. They do not want to bring bad news to management.

> **RULE:** If you want to gage employee sentiment, survey them in straight talk.

> **RULE:** If you want honest employee survey answers, act on them.

So the dilemma with HR departments, in my opinion, is that many have stopped providing services related to employment and have become employee adversaries. They seem to have their own agenda that may or may not be in the interest of the business. Unfortunately, I suspect that many HR departments in the U.S. are like my company's. There are a lot of Catberts out there.

Employee Relations

I just heard on the radio that a Canadian research organization ranked major Canadian corporations in ethical behavior. What is the most ethical corporation in Canada? The researchers ranked companies in about five categories and one was "employee relations." It struck me that this is probably what personnel and human resource departments should do. They should have a mission statement (this is another consultant gift), which includes a statement such as, "To strive to make relations and communications between employees and management open, amicable and in the interest of the business." They should make every effort to determine if any problems exist in employee/management dialog, in pay, in interpersonal relations, in their work environment – anything that could have a negative effect on the business. Large companies need an advocate for employees.

When my last employer eliminated their employee communication systems (suggestions, etc.), they instituted an ombudsman function, which was supposed to help employees solve employee and workplace problems. The ombudsman would not work on a problem; merely give you the phone number of the appropriate manager to call. In my old company, we all knew that to complain to any boss about any problem is career suicide. So, if you want to be number one in the next downsizing, call the ombudsman and make it happen.

> **RULE:** If you want honest feedback from employees, it must be anonymous.

If I were the CEO of a corporation or large organization, I would encourage the use of anonymous "dialogs" to appropriate managers. It would be part of a manager's job duties to maintain such a system and act when action is clearly needed. I submitted details of such a system to the top managers of my company and received no reply.

> **RULE:** The lack of feedback does not make problems disappear.

In summary, large companies and organizations should establish an employee relations function with a focus on addressing issues and concerns of its employees in all matters that are outside of the scope of immediate supervision. This function should have corporate funding (individual business units) and its members should be trained in psychology, arbitration, communications, and ethics. They should have had work experience on the factory floor as well as management. So you probably cannot hire the right people from a college, but you can find them from within and train them. In my company, people selected as "Advisers" would be likely candidates as employee relations workers. Union leaders may be likely candidates in unionized organizations.

An essential part of a successful employee relation's function would be to develop methods for advocacy. How does an employee bring a perceived problem to the attention of somebody who will take action? What does an employee do when an immediate supervisor will take punitive action against an employee who identifies a potential problem? What do employees do about an incompetent manager? What do employees do about an environmental infraction? What do employees do about coworker stealing? These kinds of issues must be dealt with without acknowledging the employee expressing concerns. It can be done. It must be done.

> **RULE:** If you want to root out problems, you
> must protect the whistle-blower.

Hiring - As suggested in my exit essay, I am of the opinion that the hiring function should be removed from Personnel or Human Resources Departments. Just the concept that a department can select the best candidates for a position and business that they know nothing about is preposterous. I could never hire a nurse. I have spent my life as an engineer working on the factory floor. I would have no idea if a candidate is qualified or a complete fraud. But, there are human resource companies who specialize in identifying nursing talent. The same situation exists for every profession, trade and skill. There are companies who specialize in recruiting metallurgists, chemists, structural engineers, mathematicians, statisticians – you name it. They know the field and can supply a business unit with a list of qualified candidates.

> **RULE:** If you want to hire a qualified accountant
> (or chemist, or whatever), go to a
> recruiting firm specializing in that
> profession.

Large companies only need to have a coordination function to direct a business wanting to hire to the appropriate recruiting company. The coordination function should also develop techniques to be used by business units in evaluating the suitability of screened candidates.

Benefits - The other function that does not need to be done by human resource departments is design company benefit programs. As is the case with hiring, there are commercial companies who do nothing but design and manager benefit programs. A company has only to select a plan – like buying a car. These people can continually alter benefits packages to be competitive with peers. My last employer farmed out benefits to retirees to one of these service providers and it seems to work. At least I can get a person on the phone, a feat not possible in the company's human resource department.

> **RULE:** Leave benefit packages to companies who have benefit management as their business.

Nobody is ever satisfied with benefits. We want it all. We want everything every other company offers. We want free legal service. We want free daycare. We want company cars.

Employees are insatiable. Give them what the market requires and change packages as necessary. The use of benefit purveyors will free top management from the nitty-gritty of this hopeless necessity and let them focus on the business.

Summary – My one in-depth encounter with my company's human resource department opened my eyes to what was happening in this department. I went up the line to the 16th floor of corporate headquarters so I got a vivid picture of operations at every level. It was not a pretty sight. I saw a lot of nasty people, some incompetent people and I saw a department not producing value; not contributing to the bottom line.

Instead of a costly collection of Catbert's, I propose outsourcing hiring, benefits and related personnel functions to companies who specialize in managing these matters. Companies should replace personnel and human resource functions with an employee relations department, which will truly be the advocate of employees.

CHAPTER 11:   Company Communications

Communicate What?

There are many different forms of communications in business and industry and all are important to business success. Communications is the sharing of information and ideas with others. In industry, this means managers communicating down the authority chain, employees and low-level managers communicating upward to their mangers, communicating business conditions to investors, communicating product/service advantages to customers (advertising), communicating to governments and regulatory bodies conformances to laws and regulations and communication sideways within the company among team mates, among groups, among divisions. Thus, a business needs communication systems that work in four directions: up, down, sideways and out. The following are some examples:

UP	DOWN	SIDEWAYS	OUT
Problems	Management directions	Team meetings	Technical publications
Suggestions	Employee meetings	Informal reports	Press releases
Ideas	Published rules	Formal reports	Advertisements
Reports	Published standards	Oral presentations	Photo opportunities
Surveys	Memos	Phone meetings	Interviews
Business results	Training/teaching	Video conferences	Tax returns
Staffing conditions	Benefits	Training/teaching	Environmental regulation conformance
Union issues	Appearance	Newsletters	Quality & annual reports
Body language	Union offers	Appearance	Benefits information
Spoken word	Body language	Body language	Newsletters
e-mail	Spoken word	Spoken word	Spoken word
	e-mail	e-mail	e-mail
			Internet
			Web page

I mentioned appearance in two columns. How a person dresses, combs his or her hair and "maintains" him or her self communicates personality traits. Dressing down is currently the rage in U.S. industry. Employees come to work in everything from shorts to pajamas. Male managers communicate that they are down-to-earth people by never wearing suits, only business casual (many dress like slobs). Fortunately, most women managers in my old organization did the opposite. They dressed nicely, usually in suits (thank you).

Getting back to communications, the problem addressed in this chapter is that in my company, communications was woefully lacking. I suspect a similar situation exists in most large U.S. organizations. As a worker on the factory floor, I had no idea of what was happening in the business outside of the cluster of cubicles called "my department." In fact, I really had no idea what anybody in the department did outside of my four-member team. I used to write reports religiously or projects, but I almost never received written reports on activities and projects of my teammates.

So what? Poor communications is costly to most businesses. At my level, I witnessed as many as four different groups perform similar studies (very expensive studies) on the same problem. Nobody communicated to the team that they were doing these things. Improper communications cost my company almost a billion dollars in a lawsuit lost mostly because of memos showing that engineers were reverse engineering a competitor's product. The memos implied that we were copying the competition, but this was not at all the case. However, the memos had sloppy wording that was twisted by lawyers into a loss in court. In 2002, the media announced that the Attorney General sued a brokerage firm for dishonest financial dealings and won a 100-million dollar award based upon damaging verbiage in subpoenaed e-mails. One carelessly-worded spoken sentence has cost very important government officials their jobs. Poor communications with unions have caused costly strikes. In my company, failure to communicate on discrimination claims has resulted in very costly lawsuits. So, communications are very important and they need to be improved in most U.S. corporations.

The objective of this chapter is improved communications in all directions and all forms: written, spoken, visual (appearance, body language), and less business losses from careless, misdirected or just lacking communications. This chapter will use my exit essay on the subject to point out problems at a typical large company and then discuss how a company might improve written, spoken and visual communications.

Typical Communication Problems

One of the most annoying forms of communications that was practiced by my last employer was telephone messages from the CEO distributed to all 50,000+ employees. Some were quite long and I never remembered any of them, so they did not reach me. There is a rule of thumb that says that people retain 80% of what they see, but only 5% of what they hear. We only have two ways of receiving information – sight and hearing and people who study these things may say that the percentages are different than my estimates, but most will agree that sight is more effective than hearing. I am writing this at 10:00 AM and I remember many things that I have seen this morning, but I remember nothing of what I heard and I was "listening" to the radio from 6:00 AM to 9:00 AM and I received several minutes of instructions for the day from my wife. I have no idea what she said or what the news commentators said on the public radio news – which I heard at least three times. Am I weird? Yes, but I think that I am not an exception to the seeing is more effective than hearing. And this is probably why I feel that my company's use of the phone to convey directives from the CEO is ineffective. A consultant must have told company managers that talking over the phone gives your dumb-as-a-rock employees the illusion that you called them personally to convey this information.

> **RULE:** Avoid cascaded recorded phone messages to employees. They are as effective as those from phone solicitors.

There were additional communication failings with my last employer and I will try to bring them out. I do this to point out to others what seems to work and what does not.

Exit Essay: *Employee Communications – A View from the Factory Floor*

The company used to have an employee communications system that I feel was as good as possible. There was a formal suggestion system to give financial rewards to employees who visualized and implemented changes in their workplace that saved money or increased quality. We had a "dialog" system where any employee could send an anonymous concern to any manager and expect a written reply. There was an "open door" policy that permitted any employee to talk with a manager about any subject without negative consequences.

In the manager-down direction, we used to have quarterly or semi-annual meetings with the division manager in small work groups. We got to know our division director as well as our immediate supervisor. We used to report (each person) on what we were working on and we would learn immediately from the director's response if we were working on the right things. Department communications to employees took the form of periodic meetings to discuss subjects that affected us. Communication with the big managers was as it is today, usually letters to all employees or an occasional large meeting in a 3000-seat auditorium.

I felt that we had very good communications in both directions. In addition, at most company plants, the production superintendents, division directors and other bosses above line supervisor level ate lunch together on long communal tables in the superintendent's lunchroom, which was near the plant manager's office. Top technical managers also ate in the superintendent's lunch. Eating together gave managers an opportunity to form an opinion on each other and to learn about recent problems or successes. I used to work on many problems that were identified to my director at lunch. These lunches seemed to be an ideal way to get collaboration in a large organization (The plant where I worked had over 20,000 employees at that time).

Upward and downward communication changed dramatically (for the worse, in my opinion) over the past twenty years or so. In the upward direction, the suggestion system was abolished (I guess we have no ideas anymore), the "Dialog" system was abolished (managers no longer care about our concerns), and the superintendent's lunch was eliminated because big bosses are too busy to eat lunch or talk with their peers. The open-door policy has become the out-the-door policy to those who dare try it. Upward communications has been reduced to an annual employee survey called the "People Survey." This survey is designed and administered by an outside consulting company. The survey results always show that most employees are dissatisfied with most aspects of company management and nothing, but nothing, has ever been done (as far as I can see) to improve poor employee satisfaction. Overall employee satisfaction has hovered at about 40% for the past ten years or so and thus, company managers have deemed that level "normal."

Downward communications has been mostly reduced to awkwardly relayed telephone messages from upper management and occasional e-mail messages from upper and not-so-upper management. There are regular meetings with immediate supervisors in most departments, but regular meetings usually stop there. The quarterly project meetings with our division director have ceased and now we hardly know the names of the "big bosses," and for sure they do not know our names. In our department, attendance at town meetings with company executives is restricted to selected individuals. For about two years, the manager of my organization conducted breakfast and lunch meetings open to all on a first come basis. These were a significant attempt to get employee input and he should be commended for them. However, the venue is such that he can only deal with very generic problems and there is no discussion of technical problems. This is what is most lacking (in my opinion). The big bosses are not giving us technical direction. We need specifics. What can we do in our department to improve the company's business? We can't restructure the company debt; we can't reduce inventories; we can't lower our capital spending (capital spending in our department went to zero two years ago). We could put more effort into our work with a particular manufacturing department; we could solve the product swelling problem; we could concentrate on solving the CO_2 propellant problem. Somebody in fairly high management has to give us his or her technical priorities. Then we in *engineering can help with what we do. Similarly, workers in the packaging department need to know what they can do to improve their contribution to company profits.*

In the area of written documentation on projects and studies, there is a trend to do none. Technical reports are not required or encouraged in most R&D departments and department engineering offices. In fact, in many areas they are discouraged. The results of million-dollar research studies often reside in a non-archived, undecipherable mess in computer team suites (in my experience). Formerly, we wrote formal and informal project reports that were archived. We also used to hold informal seminars to share and implement project results. Apparently, nobody in company management sees value in documenting eight hundred million dollars of annual research work and sharing successes with other units. In addition to not documenting project work, I think that the company has a huge problem with written test plans. There are countless testing steps in the development and manufacture of our products. Most test plans are so poorly written that often there is no value-derived from the millions of dollars that the company spends on testing. Acronyms are the root cause of many undecipherable test plans. Recently, somebody showed me a copy of the official list of the company's acronyms that exist on the company's intranet. As I recall, it was 70 pages long. There were acronyms that had as many as 20 different meanings. Essentially, most employees have never been trained in how to write reports or any other forms of written documentation.

In summary, I believe that poor communications is a significant company weakness. It occurs in upward and downward modes. Employees can no longer voice their concerns on any subject because the "Dialog" has been abandoned. Employees cannot get credit for their ideas because the suggestion system has been abolished. Employees hardly know any bosses above their immediate supervisor because there are no face-to-face meetings. Town meetings are mostly pep talks that paint a distorted picture of all of the company's business status. They miss the mark on producing concentrated effort on our part on key problems. Finally, written communications are sorely lacking and those that we have are often poorly written. The solution to these problems is an overall review of communication policy by a task force charged with general improvement to produce business results. We used to have a corporate manual that documented what constitutes proper and useful written documents. The company probably needs to revive this manual. Town meetings should be used to distill the messages of top managers into actionable items. Tell us specifically where we should be directing our efforts at every level. In addition, it probably would not hurt to have the training department teach on technical communications – my opinion.

I never got a reply to this essay. It is as if there was a huge vacuum above my immediate supervisor. All of these people are too busy to reply to problems or concerns from workers on the factory floor. Most managers at my company, ones important enough to have a secretary, carry with them a printout of their computer calendar showing meetings as the bulk of each day. It almost seems like they are afraid to sit in their office and write, study, or just think. Most manager meetings are not productive or associated with the business. We could see managers' calendars on the computer and the titles on meetings would be something like:

8 – 9	Computer upgrade meeting
9 – 10	Business Essentials (a consultant talk)

10 – 11	Review burden budget
11 – 12	Review new web page
1 – 2	Meet with TP team
2 – 3	Meet with safety coordinator
3 – 4	Meet with finance department on expense account problem
4 – 5	Meet with secretary on office layout

The director of engineering, my old boss, almost never met with anybody on technical matters. Her day was filled with burden meetings, meetings where attendees were all charging the company's cost of doing business rather than to work traceable to product/sales. Why so many unproductive meetings? In this case, I feel that this situation existed because most managers did not have the training and knowledge to deal with technical matters.

> **RULE:** Only attend meetings with a published agenda and identified business goals.

Finally, the elimination of project reviews by managers (above immediate supervisor) was particularly damaging in the department where I ended my industrial career. At the end, the department had $600,000 to spend on improvement projects. Essentially, this money was used to fund Internet vacation searches, noon-hour trips to the company gymnasium, and personal phone calls. The managers never asked for a report on what was done with the money, so it was given to friends of the boss and used for bogus projects; projects that did not exist and produced no business results.

> **RULE:** Managers need to take the time to review all project work in their area.

How to Improve Written Communication

In this era of personal computers, there is a trend to let all documents reside on a computer. My old company issued an edict that all formal reports must exist only in electronic form. This is done to make the job easier for the support staff that file and retrieve documents, but it increases the time and cost of producing documents by a factor of ten if the documents contain anything but words in sentences and paragraphs. Graphs, tables of data, photos, and drawings must somehow be manipulated to get into a document and this can be extremely time consuming.

One summer, I decided to teach myself computer-aided machine design (CAD). My youngest son built me a computer to do the job and my plan was to hire my niece, who was an engineering student, to learn the system and then teach me. She did her part, but the plan failed when she tried to teach me. Each day I would give her some hand-drawn sketches of machine assemblies or parts and go to work. She worked out of my home office. When I came home, the drawings were always completed – nice and neat – computer generated. When she tried to teach the system to me, I learned to my dismay that the 3-D sketch that I made in ten to fifteen minutes would take at least four hours to do on the CAD terminal. After a few CAD ventures on my part, I decided that my time was too valuable to be consumed by converting perfectly legible sketches into a computer document. So, to this day, I "outsource" computer conversion of words and thoughts. I only write e-mails on the computer. (Mostly because "wizard assisted" software has made writing on the computer horrid. A wrong keystroke can cost you an hour or sometimes eight hours. It will cause you to lose a document or not let you write the way you want with indents, listings and the like. (The word processing software that came with my new computer four months ago is unmitigated garbage – my opinion; forgive the angry departure.)

In my last work group, everybody had to type all documents, forms, presentations, etc. while the department secretary did no typing, only setting up the supervisor's meetings and talking about her personal life to others. Needless-to-say, this kind of situation is unethical, but the worst effect is to make it harder for engineers and technicians to document their work. They had to do all of the typing, scanning, printing, reviewing and editing on their own. We had no help. The same situation existed for documents to be archived at the corporate level. Computers have allowed transmittal of secretarial work to engineers, scientists and managers; the people who should be directing the company.

> **RULE:** Do not use a computer unless there is a business case for its use.

Computers, in many cases, have made it more time consuming to create written documentation of projects and programs and this should not be allowed to happen. I recommend a test on whether you should type a document or generate a drawing yourself: Ask – Can I put this message or idea on paper and save time and money by having someone else make it more presentable? If the answer is "yes" then do not do it yourself.

> **RULE:** If someone else can do it, do not do it yourself.

This will remove the "I don't have time' excuse for putting off written documentation.

Another common excuse for not documenting work or making written communications is "I am not a good writer." Only professional writers are good. The rest of us are hacks, but that is not a valid reason for not communicating in writing. A reading audience expects correct spelling and reasonable grammar. All computer word-processing programs now check both. So use them.

> **RULE:** Always check documents for correct spelling and reasonable grammar.

Writing is an acquired skill. If you do little or none, you will never become proficient. The surest way to create documents that do not hurt your reputation or credibility is to have everything that will see significant distribution reviewed by a trusted employee or coworker. Invariably, he or she will find things that need correction. And by correction, I do not mean suggesting different words to say the same thing. This is not a review. This is nit picking, so select another reviewer, one who only flags real problems. Documents do not need to be perfect, only reasonable.

> **RULE:** Always have your writing reviewed for errors and inappropriate statements by a trusted person.

I suggest a self-review on e-mails, but do not ignore it. You never know when your e-mail to a coworker may be circulated electronically to the entire corporation. I had this happen. I wrote something to the effect that a paint coating that I was evaluating seemed to have "hickies." The QC manager that I sent the e-mail to found my statement amusing and shared my e-mail with his whole division. It took me a year to live down that inappropriate word.

> **RULE:** Check your e-mails for spelling, grammar,
> and appropriate words before pressing
> "send."

I have found that I can find e-mail "boo boos" best by printing the document out. Somehow, black on white brings out errors that are completely invisible in pixels. The message here is, hone your writing skills by doing lots of it and prevent any negative effects of writing by having your documents reviewed. This will make writing easier and it will help readers because the document will read better because it was reviewed.

Finally, documents should be written right. There are established ways of writing informal and formal reports, proposals, memoranda's, etc. In fact, most word processing programs have templates for all normal business documents. Recently, I had the need to write a business plan for a small business and I discovered a template in a common program that comes free with most computers. It was really quite complete; it had all of the necessary elements and I had only to fill in the details.

> **RULE:** When you write any document, use
> established formats.

Creative writers would probably not agree with this rule. However, business documents should not read like an Ernest Hemingway novel. Business writing is concise, factual and has a purpose and objective related to the business. Creative writing usually has entertainment as an objective and traditional use of word and formats is often a key part of creative writing strategy. It is what makes it different from business writing.

> **RULE:** Business writing is business-like (no biases, no fancy phrases, and no drama) it is objective with a neutral tone.

Improving Oral Communication

I already mentioned my dislike of recorded phone messages from bosses. Recorded messages from business customers, on the other hand, are valuable and should always be promptly answered.

> **RULE:** Answer your phone messages in a timely manner.

If they are from an unsolicited salesperson, they should be discarded if you do not see a business link.

One of the commonest phone faux pas' is to take a call when you are talking with somebody else. This is just plain rude. One day, I was having lunch in a popular restaurant and I observed that at three of the five tables in the room, there were people taking cell phone calls, leaving their lunch companion sitting there looking bewildered by the cell phone owner's rudeness. There were coworkers of mine that would take phone calls when you were in their office discussing some matter. My reaction was to never go in their office. If I had a question for the person, I would call on the phone even though they sat three cubicles away.

> **RULE:** Never answer the phone when you are eating or meeting with a person.

There are phone mail systems on all business phones and they should be employed to take messages when you are preoccupied or when you need uninterrupted time to think or write.

> **RULE:** Do not let a phone dominate your time unless phone answering is your job.

Overall, I am of the opinion that phones are the lowest form of communication and their use should be discouraged. They are always an interruption; callers have no idea when you are free to talk. E-mail can completely take the place of phones (my opinion) and I advocate its use to replace phone communications. It can be real time; it can be saved; it can be converted to hard copy and they do not interrupt. You can choose when to take them and when to answer them.

> **RULE:** Deal with all e-mails in a timely manner.

> **RULE:** Be judicious about giving out your e-mail address.

Unwanted e-mails can be deleted unopened so they are not time consuming. One practice that seems to help keep my e-mail messages in control is to never give my e-mail address to anybody or companies that sell by cold calling. I never give it to technical societies who could sell the list. I guard its distribution the same way I guard my credit card number.

I recommend using e-mail and phone messages only for transient information. If you wish to communicate a directive, plan, or schedule, hard copy is usually more user-friendly. Besides, more e-mail systems will not allow extended storage of e-mails. My company did a "data dump" on anything older than thirty days. My current e-mail system limits my storage to two megabytes. A few photos eat this up fast.

Personal conversations up, down, sideways and out are a big part of business communications. We usually have mostly one-on-one meetings with our immediate supervision. Team meetings are the common way of executing projects these days. The secret to effective person-to-person communications is to be a good listener. Mostly keep your mouth shut and work at digesting what is being communicated. Conversely, you must develop techniques to shut down blabbermouths. Sometimes you need to be blunt and say, "Ralph, you have dominated the discussion; can we hear from the other team members now?"

> **RULE:** Be a good listener, but do not allow a conversation to be dominated.

Oral presentations to groups is another big part of communications, but they must be done right to get the desired results. In materials engineering, my field, most oral presentations are made with assistance from visual aids; slides, overheads, videos, projected computer "slides," computer meetings, even telephone presentations. All too often, well-intentioned speakers use visual aids that contain too much and have a negative effect on the message.

> **RULE:** Only use visual aids that summarize.

I had a supervisor who invariably in our monthly meeting used overheads made from a full page of typing and he used to uncover the typing line by line for us because we were too stupid to see the entire page at once. Needless-to-say, these kinds of visual aids should be avoided. Word slides should contain no more than two or three concise statements. Remember that their purpose is to simplify, not complicate your message.

Delivery, of course, is another significant part of oral presentations. If you stumble and are nervous, and use mannerisms such as "well," "like," "man," etc., you will annoy your audience and void your message. Effective public speaking is like effective writing, it is a learned skill. It must be practiced and continually improved.

> **RULE:** Oral presentations need concise
> visual aids and smooth delivery.

Sincerity in your message is usually the best aid to making an effective presentation. Believe in what you are telling others.

Communicating by Appearance

When managers address a group of employees or speak in front of public audiences, they should look like managers. Appropriate appearance conveys the message that a person respects the people that are being addressed. A fallout of the "American demise of structure and order" that has occurred over the past twenty years or so, is sloppiness in appearance at work. I have seen high school teachers wearing shorts, a tee shirt and destroyed sneakers. I have been in the audience when the CEO addressed a gathering of thousands in a hanging-out shirt that looked slept in, and an ugly tie sloppily tied. I have been in meetings with a woman vice president with a skirt so tight and short that I felt like a gynecologist. I have no recollection of the message delivered by these people, but I can tell you that I formed an indelible, negative opinion of the integrity of the speaker. Sloppification of America does not stop at the factory fence. It is everywhere. Women attend church in shower togs. Men come in lawn-mowing apparel. The message that they deliver to me is they are people of low esteem with emotional problems. Of course this may not be the case at all, but it is incontrovertible that appearance communicates personality traits.

RULE: Dress to communicate a positive message.

In my company, the dress code diminished when the business consultants told company officers that they should address employees in long-sleeve white shirts with a tie for executive committee and up and without for lower managers. The sleeves must be rolled up. I suspect that the managers told the gullible managers that this communicates that the manager is one of the workers. He or she labors in shirtsleeves just like the person on the punch press. This is "Dilbertonian Behavior" on the part of managers and we employees on the factory floor usually sigh: "Oh no; not another jerk."

RULE: Managers need to wear a suit, shirt, and tie.
The bigger the boss, the better the suit.

I started my career wearing an open collar white shirt with my name embroidered on the pocket – above my pen-filled pocket protector. The company used to offer these white shirts to professionals and managers for less than three dollars. They created a dress code by subsidizing what managers wanted support staff to wear. During the white shirt and tie years (1960's – 1970's), I non-conformed by wearing turtlenecks, a sport coat and a necklace. Then I wore a shirt, tie and sport coat, and for the last fifteen years or so, I wore a suit and tie. My non-conforming attire was intended to communicate to coworkers and managers that I am different from the other employees. It probably communicated "jerk," but only a year or so into my suit era, I discovered that wearing suits was a huge time and money savings. I had a business case for wearing them.

When I was in business casual mode, I used to spend up to ten minutes each morning picking out clothing items that matched. Also, I used to spend a lot of money buying shirts, slacks, ties and sport coats that would intermingle. When I switched to suits, the ten-minute morning selection ordeal was reduced to ten seconds. I would have my suit pants on one rack; I picked one; that determined what I would wear. All my ties were neutral to go with all suits. I bought at least one good suit on sale each year and they never wear out. So it cost me only about $150.00 per year for clothing. Shirts and ties, of course, were father's day gifts. My business casual costs were at least four times this number.

RULE: Wear suits to save time and money.

The only problem with wearing suits is that I retired with eighteen. Now I look like a jerk mowing the lawn in a business suit and tie.

Summary

This may be one of the most important chapters in this book, but length restrictions preclude more specifics. We started this chapter with a tabulation of up, down, sideways and out modes of communications that managers must be concerned with. All of the communication channels in our tabulation are important and each and every manager should establish a strategy on how to do each.

RULE: Develop a communications strategy.

An action item that can be taken in developing a strategy and improving communications is to survey employees whenever possible. When you make a formal presentation, pass out a simple survey to gather audience response. Survey employees on written and other forms of communications. Find out what works for your particular situation. Include what seems to work in your strategy and then develop a program to continually improve their effectiveness. By all means also do this with customers and investors.

Communications sell products and services; good communications with employees prevents labor problems; good communications within your technical staff promotes innovation and decreases time to market.

RULE: Business success is dependent on effective communications.

CHAPTER 12:   Diversity

All of American industry seems to waltz to the same tune. I wish I knew from where the tune was emanating. Maybe then I could figure out what is behind the tune that has clouded America's managers reasoning since about 1998. Every English-speaking person knows the word to mean accommodation of differences. A rain forest may accommodate many species of plants and creatures. A lake may have a diverse population of fish. Older cities have diversity in housing types and our planet contains diversity in people. There are countless cultures, countless personalities, and countless ways of dressing and different skin colorations. Skin color options are few; they only range from white, to yellow, to black. The six billion people on this planet are all different, all unique and no two are absolutely identical. Even "identical" twins have different persona. Our culture and persona is determined by birth circumstance. None of us had a choice in selecting our parents. We are all different - we are diverse.

"Diversity" has become a program in American industry and many other U.S. organizations. The stated objective of the program is a workforce that consists of all types of people, all colors, all cultures, and all personas. Unfortunately, as practiced, it is selective hiring and promotion of people because of birth circumstance or sexual orientation. Somebody in corporate management has assigned "diversity" status to people born in certain places, born to certain parents, born in certain cultures; there are favored birth circumstances. I do not understand the reasoning and ethics of making sexual persuasion a basis for employment, but it is part of U.S. corporate diversity directives. People who like a particular type of sex are to be given preference in hiring and promotion.

The diversity program at my last place of employment was devouring the plant that I worked at. It was a key manufacturing function for the corporation, its largest and oldest plant. Diversity started with slogans, "We must have a winning inclusive culture." Then it progressed to force fitting women and African Americans into key management positions. When I left the company, diversity had become the primary focus of the management at the plant where I worked. This in turn resulted in greatly diminished attention to making products and to product quality. Diminished product quality and no new products in turn led to reduced sales which led to shrinking market share which led to diminishing stock prices. The company was faltering because they were ignoring the business. Key technical people were told not to work on product problems. Diversity initiatives are "job one." At the time of writing this chapter, there was an article in the local newspaper reporting (in the same article) that Wall Street analysts downgraded the company's stock for the second time in a week, but a diversity web site ranked the company second among fifty top companies. The same article went on to remind readers that the company's headquarters were picketed two weeks earlier by African Americans. They called the company unfair to African Americans. So in my opinion, diversity programs can have a negative effect on both business and employee morale. I think that this situation exists wherever diversity programs are forced on employees. They are fundamentally discrimination and discrimination is wrong. That is the diversity problem.

It is the purpose of this chapter to present a view from the factory floor (mine) of my company's diversity program. The objective of my discussing diversity is, to put it bluntly, to stop these programs. They are discrimination and they are diametrically opposed to their purported objective.

This chapter will discuss my exit essay on the subject and then explore the ethics of diversity and the business case for diversity in U.S. manufacturing.

The Seriousness of the Problem

When I left my last employer, they had a chief diversity officer (a vice-president) and the organization that I worked for fired the HR director (a woman) and brought in an African American woman to institute "conversion" to a diverse workforce. In other words, fire all employees who did not fall into their predetermined diverse workforce. They had percentage goals on each type of people that they want working for the company. The plant leadership team at that time had the following ethnic/gender mix.

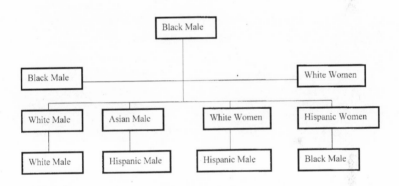

Nine out of the eleven leaders were "diverse" by company definition. I had worked at this plant for thirty-eight years and knew many people. I only recognized three of the eleven, two white males and one white female. I suspect all of the other people were "brought in" to ensure that the proper race, gender, and sexual persuasion were in force at all levels. Almost all department and higher meetings were devoted to discussing culture change and diversity.

Meanwhile, our significant company competitors were taking five percent market share from us per year. Our significant competitor was Japanese. Needless-to-say, they did not spend their time changing their workforce to achieve gender, race, and sexual persuasion quotas. I have visited their facilities in Tokyo and I can say with 100% certainty that they did not have a diverse workforce by my company's definition. The workforce in Japan was probably 90% male and 99.9% Japanese. They were focusing on the business and "cleaning our clock" as they say. They are being so successful that I suspect that my company will be out of business by 2010 unless there is a refocus on the business. I suspect that this situation is epidemic in the U.S. only the prime competitors may be from China or another third world-country where there is no preoccupation with diversity. Those who totally ignore the business like my company will also probably disappear by 2010. This is how serious the problem is.

Here is my exit essay on diversity. It was not answered and it was probably not read.

Exit Essay: *Diversity – A View from the Factory Floor*

I touched on the subject of diversity in other essays, but it is such an important subject that I think that it deserves its own essay. Diversity as practiced in the company appears to me to be nothing but a program to increase the number of "defined" minorities to some prescribed ratio. Somebody at a very high level provided the definition of minorities, and it appears that target minorities are: African American, Hispanic, female, Asian and people who advertise their sexual proclivities. I suspect that there is a document someplace that states the company's numerical goals in each area.

In my opinion, this type of diversity initiative is simply discrimination. The company is offering special treatment to select groups of people. If you are not one of the select, you have no opportunity to be hired or to be promoted if you were an employee prior to the diversity initiative. Diversity seems to be rationalized by management two ways:

1. *Diversity is a way to redress discrimination in the United States in previous generations.*
2. *A workforce consisting of a prescribed ratio of selected minorities will be more productive and innovative than a workforce without a designated number of minorities.*

I have discussed these rationalizations with quite a number of company managers and they seem to be united in their stance and that these are sufficient reasons for practicing discrimination. The remainder of this essay contains my comments on these points as well as my thoughts on why this company's workforce composition will never mirror our customer base (a goal stated in the Company's "Culture" posters).

Diversity as redress for past discrimination *– I was told by a company HR manager that it is proper for the company to hire minorities preferentially because "minorities have not had equal opportunities in the past." I obtained the very distinct impression that this person was hired by the company with the mission of recruiting minorities to become managers. The company somehow believes that placing minorities in leadership roles will somehow absolve American industry of past discrimination in hiring. The company is a worldwide corporation owned by thousands of people, many of them minorities. These owners have entrusted company leadership with the task of* growing their investment. Job one of company leaders is to make profits and pay dividends to owners. Their job is not to right social wrongs committed by others. I wish that I could undo slavery, the exploitation of Native Americans, the Communist repression of personal freedoms in Poland, and the environmental damage produced by clear cutting forests in Oregon. I cannot, and it would be foolhardy, even immoral, for me to use my family's financial resources to launch a quixotic campaign to right these wrongs. Long-past wrongs cannot be righted by present generations. Also, it is never advisable to try and right a wrong with another wrong – discrimination.

Diversity produces business success – We are told that a group of employees consisting of the right number of the company's selected minorities will produce results not possible with our present employee makeup, which is mostly white male. The different approach brought to the problem by each cultural background is what makes diverse teams so successful. I agree that teams comprised of people with different work experiences and skills can often produce synergies that may not happen with monolithic teams. However, a team with membership based upon birth circumstance and sexual proclivity makes no sense to me. Like it or not, making consumer products is a technology-based business. The company with the best technology wins. Assembling a team with people with varied racial origins may produce a nice social gathering, but such a team may never have what it takes to design a new computer or solve a software problem unless team members have skills in these areas. Birth circumstance is not a substitute for knowledge, expertise, talent, and skills.

What should the company do to increase minorities in their workforce? – In my opinion, any action that is intended to give preference to any "group" is

discrimination. It is a violation of the United States'
"Equal Employment Opportunity" legislation that has been
in place for a number of years, and it should not be done.
It is also unethical. I believe that the company should
change its diversity policy to allow equal opportunity for
all. Currently, there is not equal opportunity in hiring or
promotion. Hiring and promotion recommendations now
come from secret management cliques and caucuses. Our
supervisor is retiring next week. He is being replaced by a
boss selected by I do not know who, and the person that
was secretly selected for the job has no experience or
education in our technologies. This is the current company
system. Employees have no say in who will be their leader.
I recommend that all positions be posted and that anyone
can apply for the posted positions. A department selection
committee should screen the candidates and make the final
selection. Needless-to-say, the selection committee should
be comprised of fair and competent individuals. This same
type of system should be used for new hires. The company
must move to selecting the best person for a position, not a
race, culture, or lifestyle.

Why the workforce will never mirror our customer base –
For those that argue that the company must demonstrate
that it has an affirmative action plan, I maintain that my
proposal is an affirmative action plan. Also, a more
pragmatic reason for not relying on diversity and other
affirmative action programs is that they do not work. As an
example, about fifteen years ago, one of my college alma
maters launched a massive, well-funded campaign to bring
more women and African Americans into their engineering
programs. They recruited heavily; they conducted summer
camps for high schoolers, and they offered essentially free
tuition and almost every imaginable special treatment.
This spring I visited the university and I had dinner with
the university president. He lamented to me that after

fifteen years of aggressive affirmative action they could not get numbers better than about fifteen percent female and six percent African American (with some double counting). These numbers are far short of the fifty percent female and twenty percent African American ratios that exist in our local customer base. The numbers obtained after an aggressive affirmative action program are about the same as numbers in engineering schools who did nothing. Why is this? I think that their targeted groups were just not that interested in engineering. I do mason work as a hobby, and I have observed that there are very few female masons. In fact, I have never seen one. Why? I do not know, but I suspect that women prefer that the skin on their hands not be turned into elephant hide as required by the profession. Conversely, few males become nurses. Probably because men prefer jobs that are more tool and machine oriented rather than people oriented.

My point is that the workforce in any company will probably never have the same ratio of races and cultures as their customer base. Males prefer some types of jobs; females prefer some types of jobs, and race and sexual persuasion should never even be considered. It is simply not a factor in running a business. Just as everyone can buy products from the company, so should everyone have the opportunity to work at the company.

*In summary, I believe that the company's diversity program is nothing but discrimination housed in business jargon. I also believe that any factory making anything will never have a workforce that mimics its customer base unless it is artificially created by discriminatory hiring and promotion. The only ethical way to deal with diversity is to **really** practice equal opportunity. The company needs to get rid of its secret backroom selection practices and post all positions. In addition, they must develop a non-*

*discriminatory candidate-screening process to fill
positions. The company needs to use talent as its top
selection criterion. The best talent, not a forced ratio of
preferred people will produce the best business results.
This is my opinion of diversity.*

In may not have been evident in my exit essay, but I have
not witnessed any and I mean "any," positive benefits from
all of the diversity efforts in my company. The director of
the division that I worked in was given his job because he
was a diversity, and I think that he would never even be
considered for this position based upon his skills and
accomplishments. He is absolutely not a leader; he cannot
make decisions and give direction. I participated on a team
that met with her every two weeks for about six months.
We all became completely exasperated after several
meetings because we could not pry from her what she
wanted us to do. She was the boss, but could not
communicate what she wanted from us. Certainly, this
person would not be considered for any leadership position
if she were not a "diversity." She was an intelligent person
and acted friendly to us, but she was not a leader. This
same situation probably exists in many diversity
management appointments. They do not have the
leadership credentials required for the job.

RULE: Make managers only from staff who have
demonstrated their ability to lead.

One of the most blatant examples of "diversity destruction"
in my company was the appointment of a lesbian diversity
to the position of manager of the company's construction
department. This woman was a secretary, then an
administrative assistant and then a manager. I suspect that
she never even saw a construction site before she was

appointed manager. Those of us who work in engineering rely heavily on skilled trades, and we know well that most are a special breed of employees. They are very intelligent and very skilled with their hands. They know machinery and tools, and most can make anything. They communicate in technical terms. To put in a person who knows absolutely zero about this business is an affront to these skilled people. It is saying anybody can run this business. (And this is current HR philosophy – there is no need to know anything about what you manage.)

So what happened is that the construction department declined from being the best to one that was not competitive with "outside" construction departments. Much work was outsourced because they no longer have the skills and machines to compete. Many skilled trades people retired at their first opportunity and all new employees are diversity hires who maybe could become skilled workers, but there were no senior skilled workers left to train and mentor the new people. Diversity greatly diminished a key company resource.

> **RULE:** Do not denigrate employees by giving them an inappropriate manager.

The Ethics of Diversity

The "platform" of this book is business ethics. I have been promoting ethics as the criterion for all business decisions. Ethical behavior means that a person or business does what is right. People can say that people have a different opinion of what is right and wrong. I answer: Not really. In the United States, everybody does "stuff" to reduce his or her tax burden. I am currently protesting a recent reassessment on one of my houses. The town where I live reassesses all the town properties every five years and, of course, they always say that all properties increased in value. They have data that shows that only 500 or so people out of 15,000 property owners will protest. So they can, essentially, raise taxes without raising the tax rate. They increase the basis. This is perfectly legal, but not ethical. They are concealing a tax increase. They know that the average selling price of homes has not increased in the past five years - it decreased. The data is there for people to see, but the government officials know that most people will not bother to complain.

> **RULE:** People know what is "right" and what is "wrong;" do what is right.

Ethical behavior on the part of my town would be to announce a plan to reassess with a goal of increasing the taxes collected by ten percent (or whatever they want).

Ethical behavior in hiring means matching job requirements to training, education and experience of candidates. My company has a declared program to hire to achieve birth circumstance and sexual proclivity goals. The plant where I worked was in a community where eighteen percent of the population was African American. So the plant was required to bring employment of African Americans to eighteen percent. The Hispanic population was nine percent so this became the plant goal. A fraction of a percent of the population was gay, so obtaining gay employees became a mandate. Finally, fifty percent of the local population was female, so this meant fifty percent of the employees must be women. These quotas were established at a high management level and they were implemented by rising layoffs and retirement incentives to remove non-diversity. Concurrently, there was a program to only hire and promote diversities. The bottom line of their diversity quotas is that only twenty-two out of one hundred employees can be white males. Is this ethical? Is it right to remove white male employees who have devoted their entire working lives to the business and replace them with people who may know nothing of the business, but have the right gender or ethnicity.

The curious aspect of the diversity hiring and promotion plan is that it was not diverse or inclusive. It was just the opposite – it excluded most ethnicities. There are more than 150 countries on our planet and each has a different culture, sometimes color, sometimes religion, sometimes government system. The point is that African-American, Hispanic and gay are not inclusive, not diverse. Why didn't my company have a quota for Russians? Why didn't my company have a quota for Japanese? Why didn't my company have a quota for Malaysians? All of them are significant percentages of the world's population.

> **RULE:** Include all as employee candidates –
> that is diversity.

The diversity programs are simply unethical – they discriminate; they are dishonest in that managers' actions are not for business reasons; they disregard the work and efforts of long-time employees; the impugn the credibility of all managers – none ever gives an honest answer to a non-diversity, they do not respect the rights of non-diversities, they do not show consideration for others, they do not allow a differing opinion. They are the antithesis of corporate ethics.

The last point that I shall try to reinforce is that it is wrong to use American industry as a tool to redress wrongs of the past. Discrimination happened in the United States to just about every group of immigrants. When immigrants came in groups, they presented a threat to the culture of those already there so they discriminated. The Anglican majority along the east coast of the U.S. discriminated against Catholics, so they moved inward to Maryland and other places where they could lead their way of life. Of course, slaves had no choice in their immigration to the US and they were sold like property. This was wrong, but we cannot undo this wrong. It was wrong for immigrants to steal the United States from the Native Americans, but we cannot undo this wrong.

Many minorities, like the HR director at the plant where I worked, believe that retribution is due for past discrimination. Diversity programs are thought by some to be the means to retribution. Minorities will be given employment as retribution. Again, I say that this is wrong. I suspect that every person in the world is discriminated against at some time for some reason. I was discriminated against because I was of my Polish ancestry. And it still happens. When I was working in Detroit as part of my cooperative engineering training, I was told by a girl that I asked for a date that she could not go out with me because I was Polish. There was a very large Polish population at that time in the Hamtramck section of Detroit. Local non-Poles did not like having whole neighborhoods and significant number of jobs lost to immigrants. Thus they discriminated against Poles. Polish jokes continue to surface now and then. People characterized us as stupid. Now, mostly my wife does that.

I was discriminated against as a graduate student for no reason on my part. I went to a state school in a remote area of the Midwest U.S. The local population was predominately Finnish and they resented the students moving into their "pure" Finish neighborhoods. Students were not allowed in Finnish bars. And that is a big thing for college students. Both of these acts of discrimination in the U.S. occurred in the 1950's and '60's.

> **RULE:** Discrimination will never stop – it is the product of our nature. Discourage it, but do not offer the company as retribution.

My final story on discrimination: Some years ago, I visited Ernest Hemingway's home in Key West. Hemmingway left this house to his cats. When he died, he had a dozen or so cats and they were special because all had five toes on one paw. I guess four is normal. Apparently, he had one five-toed cat and eventually all his cats ended up with five toes. When I visited his house, the house and grounds were owned by about 100 cats, all with five toes on one paw. I asked a guide, "How do you keep non-Hemingway cats out of the compound? They have a great life. They have seven veterinarians on call, all the food they want and no worries." The guide said that the Hemingway cats kill stray cats that try to take up residence in the compound. Even in the animal kingdom there is a natural tendency to discriminate. It cannot be stopped by an industrial corporation, and to offer a corporation as retribution for perceived past social injustices is a complete lapse of ethics. It is cheating the owners, the stockholders; it is cheating the employees who keep the company running, and it cheats customers. Products degrade because the company's focus is elsewhere.

The Business Case for Diversity

I mentioned in my exit essay that I made a concerted effort to learn the business case for my company's diversity program. I really made an effort. Every time (and these were numerous) that I sat in an audience to get a diversity lecture, I asked the question: What is the business case for this diversity program? They invariably parroted the official company stance – "we will do all things better with a diverse workforce." I never received any data to support this contention. One slide presented at a diversity talk claimed that in the 1980's, "adaptive culture companies" increased sales by 682%, increased stock value 901%, expanded the workforce 282%, and improved net income by 756%. There was also a slide that said that GE, Chrysler, Ford and HP were examples of companies who credit their phenomenal success on diversity programs. GE recently laid off a minority friend of mine; Chrysler got sold to Mercedes; Ford Is not doing well; and HP had to merge this year to survive. I guess that I still need to see data to show the correlation between business success and a workforce with designated ratios of selected minorities and proclivities.

What does make a lot of sense is to structure marketing efforts to sell to the many cultures encountered in a worldwide market. For example, in the U.S., disposable cameras are very popular consumer items. In India, nobody would even consider disposing of a camera. They want cameras that last a lifetime. It would be a marketing faux pas to try to push these disposable cameras in India. An Indian sales activity staffed by Indians could advise on marketing to this culture. Marketing to Japanese and Chinese similarly requires an intimate knowledge of their culture. By all means, hire Chinese to market to Chinese and Japanese to sell to Japanese.

> **RULE:** Market to a culture with a sales staff
> who is of that culture.

This is not diversity - it is marketing savvy.

The greatest challenge to American industry comes from China and Japan. They are the competition to deal with in almost all products. They do not have diversity programs. In fact, I toured lots of factories in China and Japan and I never saw one person who appeared to be other than Japanese or Chinese. They do hire locals to market. Most Japanese, Korean, German, etc. car companies hire an American to head their U.S. marketing operation. Not the technical staff; not the manufacturing employees. They are focused on the business. U.S. industry seems to be focused on other matters.

> **RULE:** The company that focuses on the business will win.

Summary

Last month I attended a technical conference in Portugal with delegates invited from nineteen countries. I sat next to a delegate from South Africa at two lunches and a formal dinner, and we talked a lot about the culture changes in her country. She told me that: "A white person cannot be an employee in South Africa. They can be entrepreneurs, but not employees. This is not right, but apartheid was not right." I said nothing to this statement, but my inner reaction is: This country is doomed to failure. They are trying to redress a wrong with another wrong. Haven't we learned yet that this does not work? This is not ethical. This is not fair. This does not make business sense.

What would I do about diversity if I were a CEO of a large worldwide corporation? Hire the best qualified and promote the best qualified considering only factors relating to ability to achieve business results. I believe that individuals do not discriminate based upon race, religion, sexual persuasion, whatever, unless they are given a reason.

I have spent my professional life working in a worldwide technical community and I have never heard any of my technical colleagues even mention anything, but qualifications when it comes to technical organization leadership. There are no race, color, religion, gender, etc. barriers. There is complete absence of a person's culture or color as a consideration. This is what would happen if diversity programs were sent where they belong – back to the consultants who get rich selling them. My company spent 42 million dollars that they did not have to institute a diversity program and all it did was make old employees unhappy, even the designated minorities, and promote more discrimination lawsuits.

I would make sure that the company hired appropriate cultures to market to different cultures, but I would not force social quotas on a corporation. It is wrong.

> **RULE:** Do not establish quotas for types of employees; let everyone have equal opportunity.

My final rule on diversity:

> **RULE:** Do not let social justice programs become a business diversion.

I really believe that it was in my company. Managers were not successful in dealing with business failings, so they espoused diversity as a diversion. This is hardly ethical behavior and it can only lead to resentment, anger and hatred in employees not selected for special treatment.

CHAPTER 13: Corporate Research

Universal Problems

In manufacturing industries, research efforts lead to new products; in service industries, it leads to services. The reason why corporations dedicate a percentage of their earnings (usually 3 to 10%) to research is that new products and services are needed to keep profitable and to stay ahead of the competition. All of us have witnessed companies disappear from the face of the earth because they tried to keep going on "same old." In 2000 or thereabouts, here in the U.S. we witnessed a venerable automobile brand disappear, the Plymouth, because it did not have something special to set it apart from the other cars made by the corporation. On the other hand, we witnessed survival of the venerable Jeep, a fifty-year-old design, with mutations to sports utility vehicles and other forms.

In the service industry, almost all of the family owned diners that dotted city and town street corners were displaced by "fast food" restaurants. And they are the norm today. New guys offered customers fast service, playgrounds, toys for youths – stuff to discriminate themselves from plain family diners. The food was undoubtedly better at the family diners, but that did not matter. Customers went for the new stuff.

Research in universities used to be fundamental in nature; it was published and shared with all and universities avoided commercial applications of their research. Today, just the opposite is true. Universities require their engineering faculty to run research businesses as well as teach. They spend a great deal of their time writing proposals and to get tenure a professor should have a going research business with funding of at least $100,000 per year. This funding comes from government and industry and it buys equipment, pays for the professor's travel to conferences, sometimes the professor gives himself a salary, but most of the money goes to paying tuition and giving a stipend to graduate students.

My graduate school was paid for by one of these grants and I would not have been able to do to graduate school without them. So what is the problem? Aren't these things good? Certainly it is good to promote graduate school education and support the fundamental research that is normally done by graduate students. However, over the past twenty years or so, corporate greed has spilled over into academic institutions and their financial analysts and lawyers are encouraging the formation of university corporations who own and patent research results, equipment, and even unproven ideas. The problem that relates to industry is that it is difficult to collaborate with universities on research efforts. They control the best young intellects and university intellectual property barriers are diminishing opportunities for industry to have joint research. This is hurting U.S. industry.

Fundamental problems with in-house industrial research include: lack of focus, lack of reasonable strategy, lack of timeliness, lack of necessary competencies, and in many cases, lack of common sense. Of course I will give examples to illustrate these problems from my experience, but I suspect that most industries have the same problems. I have consulted with peer organizations of mine since I retired and I heard the same lamentations from research staff.

The purpose of this chapter is to review my research experiences and to show how staff and methods can be improved to yield more good ideas, more marketable products and services. Our objective is a more vibrant and competitive U.S. industry. We will use my exit essay on the subject as the nucleus for improvement suggestions in research strategy, research staff, and common sense research.

My Company's Problems

One of my last ditch efforts to save my company was to get an hour with the chief technical officer to make a pitch for a comprehensive study to increase the productivity of the company's research staff. I wanted to spend my final year before retirement interviewing research and engineering managers and staff on how to improve and put my results into a "white paper" that could serve as a blueprint for changing things to get more results – more home runs. The net result of my meeting was an opinion of the technical director and denial of my study proposal and a new product proposal. My opinion of the technical director is that he was aloof and not really open to differing opinions. He did not believe that there were any problems with the research staff even though company earnings and sales have been diminishing each of the three years or so that he was chief technical officer. Also, there were no home run products in the queue. He did not seem at all interested in hearing my arguments for my product. I did not get a chance to sell it. The chief technical officer came from a peer company where he was the technical officer for a small division. I got the distinct impression that he was not familiar with the long-time research thrusts of my company and was taking the company in the direction of technologies that he was more familiar with, but which were not part of his new company's mission and vision. He didn't seem to change research directions even though he changed companies. My exit essay will touch on some specifics.

Exit Essay: *The Company's Research Effort – A View from the Factory Floor*

The company's research labs were always sacrosanct. The staff was mostly Ph.D.'s, the facilities were the best, they had lots of funding, and they worked on whatever they wanted. New products emerged, but not many and we took about five years to get one into production. They did a lot of basic research. Even as late as 1990, the company had about 150 people working on "whatever." Now that the company has a chief technical officer in each of seven business units, it is not clear to me how the company's research labs, which still employ about 1500 people, work with business units. It also appears that the research labs have lowered their academic standards. I do not see many Ph.D.'s or people who behave or sound like Ph.D.'s. I do not see many scholarly reports or studies.

I sense that the company's top executives question the value derived from the hundreds of millions of dollars expended each year. I know that lots of the research funds are expended in studying environmentally mandated product changes. EPA, or some other regulatory body, bans a surfactant or solvent and the research staff has to do significant testing to find a replacement. The same testing is required every time that the purchasing department changes a feedstock supplier to reduce cost. These efforts usually produce no new revenues; their value is to try to reduce the negative effects of different feedstocks. Hardware and software research is so fragmented by individual business unit requirements that major innovations seldom occur. Research into non-core products like electronic gadgets, in my view, do not fit into the company's vision or mission. The company does not have the technical talent to be competitive in these areas. The company's research labs are staffed mostly with chemists, and we do not have the right staff to take on Sony, HP, Toshiba, and the other electronic giants.

What else can the company do to get more value from the research labs? I suggest that the company consider at a very high level what needs to be researched in each of these thrusts. The Research Labs should be redirected to work in each of product priority. Of course, there are different technical aspects of each product. There are fundamental concepts: device engineering and design, make or buy development of manufacturing methods, tool engineering (tool design), capital equipment implementation (getting equipment made), facilities engineering (getting a place for manufacturing equipment), process engineering (methods, procedures and quality). The first three responsibilities (concept, device engineering, make or by) should reside in product research and development, the department that should replace the Research Labs. The technical functions outside of product development can reside in the company's engineering division.

Universities and contract research organizations should also be explored as a way to fill technology gaps. If we need a new sensor, find Ph.D. students charged with the task and pay for their work. If we need a particular piece of software, we could solicit software developers to submit development plans and costs. We need to be nimble and find necessary talent fast. We cannot wait for research lab employees to learn how to make a needed sensor. We must get one any way we can.

Finally, the company needs to address what to do with its analytical labs. In the early days, these labs contained the company's analytical chemists. They were an autonomous division and did analytical chemistry work for the research

*labs, but they did not report directly to the head of the
research labs. They were staffed with many Ph.D.
chemists, mostly organic, and way too many technicians.
The analytical lab had a huge capital budget and they
bought every hundred- thousand-dollar piece of analytical
equipment on the market – usually several copies. They
also bought each year's upgrades. They work on whatever
they want and spend much time and money developing
special analytical procedures in case somebody needs one.*

*This division needs to be absorbed by the proposed product
research and development organization and should be
refocused to do analytical work needed for product
development and manufacturing quality control problems.
Business units and technical communities should be
surveyed for their analytical needs. The analytical
technology labs should be restructured to focus on these
needs. They should assume quality control functions that
involve analytical chemistry and assume some quality
control functions that are currently being ignored.*

*Overall, the company's analytical functions need to be
consolidated into the analytical technology labs, which are
part of product R&D. The analytical labs in individual
business units should be absorbed. Routine chemical
analyses and related tests should be outsourced to
competent analyses service companies and the analytical
technology labs should refocus on addressing the
analytical needs of our proprietary activities.*

*In summary, I am of the opinion that the company has not
gotten their money's worth out of its research labs in many
years. An important reason for this in recent times has
been the wrong kind of talent and an overly complicated
organization. The company needs to replace the research
labs with a product research and development department*

and an engineering department, which report to the Chief Technical Officer. Business unit technical staff and all engineering functions in the corporation need to be rolled into this single technical community. Staffing needs to be based upon demonstrated talent and the Executive Council needs to establish what technologies are to be pursued. A collaborative technical team can then go after clearly identified technology goals. For the shareholders' and pensioners' sake (moi) please make these goals something related to the company's mission.

*There are over six billion people in our customer base. I estimate that less than a billion of these people will **ever** be able to afford the gadgetry or have the time needed for some proposed electronic products. The company needs to spend its R&D dollars developing products for the five billion non-wired potential customers that exist worldwide. Focus R&D efforts and redirect them to fulfill the needs of the five billion people who will continue to buy-low cost consumer goods and not big-ticket products for the wealthiest fraction of the world's population – my opinion.*

I had to edit many specifics from my exit essay because they may be considered confidential information from the company's standpoint. Essentially, I was urging them to go easy in a technology field where we did not have the appropriate technical staff to be a leader. This is the common sense part of research. I witnessed a large peer manufacturing company lose their shirt by a fling into the insurance business. It sounded nice on paper. Take excess profits, buy insurance companies and they will automatically provide lots of extra profits to grow the manufacturing business. Everybody knows that insurance companies always make money. They take in exorbitant fees and never pay out claims without a court fight that the consumer can ill afford. Well, it is not necessary to go into the details, but the ending of this story is that the manufacturing company was happy to dump their insurance companies at half the purchase price. They suffered terrible losses for the ten years that they tried to be something that they were not.

> **RULE:** If you want to make money in a business, know it.

Another point that I tried to make in my exit essay was that they had some significant staff liabilities. Probably twenty percent of the research staff was analytical chemists. Of course every large company needs analytical capability, but much of this type of work is available from service providers. There were too many people doing routine analytical work and calling it research. In fact, many of the staff were technicians who learned to run analytical machines, but did not have education in the chemical principals surrounding "their instrument."

> **RULE:** A research organization should never have machine operators.

We had technicians who would do nothing else but run a particular instrument, for example, a tensile tester. If you asked that person to do a coating thickness test, they would refuse. The company was not unionized, but the staff has a culture of "I only do what I want to do." And, this was okay with management. They got raises each year for working sometimes only a few hours per week. If there was no work for his or her instrument, they amused themselves with personal business or surfing the Internet.

One time I tried to find out from human relations how many mechanical, chemical and electrical engineers the company had in its technical staff. I learned that it was not possible to obtain this data. They did not have it. Employees are given a human relations title like engineer, scientist, technician, etc. and there was no correlation between human relations titles and education and training. For example, we had an engineer in our department with no formal education beyond high school. In fact, I doubt that this person even completed high school. The human relations department had a firm policy that education, training, and competency was not a consideration for any company position. This was part of the staffing problem. People gravitate to a research job and do whatever they can to keep this job. They lobby to do "their test" on all products whether or not it is producing valuable information.

> **RULE:** Beware of unnecessary testing; have a
> plan to monitor value.

The final staffing concern that I alluded to in my exit essay was the dearth of Ph.D.'s. Hiring technical people who have completed a doctorate does not insure competency, but it sure helps the screening process. In fact, I mentioned previously (I think) that I am of the opinion that all technical professionals should have advanced degrees and non-degreed (baccalaureate or better) people should not be made engineers or scientists unless they prove understanding of technical fundamentals. For example, successful completion of a professional engineering licensing exam would qualify a person with no formal education for ranking as a technical professional.

> **RULE:** Technical staff should have appropriate
> formal education.

Of course, research managers should be eminent scientists. They should be models of behavior, work ethics, and productivity for the technical staff. They also should have their eminence in a field related to company objectives. An eminent biologist is likely to be not very productive as research manager of a metal stamping company.

> **RULE:** Research managers should have training and experience that compliments company objectives.

Establishing a Research Strategy

Most companies claim that they have a research strategy, but my consulting and networking activities suggest to me that most companies have a fuzzy research strategy. They seem to vacillate with what is in vogue that quarter or that year. Use of fiber optics and light for the transmission of digital data was all the rage two years ago. Many U.S. companies decided that this is the most profitable technology and they aimed their research dollars in that direction. Photonics research activities popped up in many places. Even the U.S. government jumped on the bandwagon with research centers. Four years ago, the same thing happened with small things. Research centers were formed on nano-particles, nano-network, nano-tribology, nano-mechanisms (MEMS – microelectronic mechanical systems). This year, the word is "bio." Biodegradable, biophilic, bio-clean, bio-active are terms used for research thrusts aimed at making plastics from organic feedstocks, for detergents that come from oranges, foods that contain no biological agents.

I attended a technical meeting with a researcher from a government agency and he intimated in his talk that the government of the U.S.A. will not fund any research project unless the title includes at least one of three prefixes: "bio," "nano," or "info."

> **RULE:** Beware of fad research. It can eat your funds and produce no profits.

At this writing, the photonics business is essentially moribund and several photonic research facilities that I am familiar with have been shuttered. Ten or fifteen years ago, we witnessed billions of dollars in research funds go down the toilet looking for super conducting wires. Laboratory curiosities created most research fads. Gullible research managers created the huge losses of research dollars. They were "suckered in" by golden-tongued research-sales people. It is reasonable to pursue super conductors if you are a wire manufacturer or company who would make a lot of money through the application of high electrical conductivity materials, but if you are a detergent manufacturer, it does not make sense to squander research dollars on a technology that does not apply to your business.

> **RULE:** Direct your research, even risky, fundamental research, to apply to your core business.

In other words, all research should be aimed at what you do or what you want to do. If you want to be the number one manufacturer of hot tubs, then do research into materials and devices that apply to the hot tub business.

> **RULE:** Establish a long-term research objective.

One of the many consultants that my company hired to fix us had a good philosophy that I think can apply to research: "Measure and track what you want to change or control." This could be a rule; it belongs to one of the consultants and I would give him or her credit, but I cannot remember for sure, which one it came from. So here it is:

> **RULE:** "Measure and track what you want to change or control"

If a company wants to develop a device to sense water temperature and computer control it to plus or minus 1 degree Celsius, then the task should be assigned to a team and put into bite-sized steps that can be tracked for completion. Do not just track spending. Track results towards the research objective. Sometimes, the objective can be decades away. That is a bit much in my estimation, but I know of a government nuclear fusion research project that has until 2020 to demonstrate parity of power in and power out and they have been at this project for about twenty years already. They track percent of power in as their measure of progress. Most manufacturing companies do not have deep enough pockets for this kind of timeline, but the message is to track even very long-term projects. Establish measures for all projects and track results.

Next, a company needs to identify the products or services that they need to differentiate themselves from the competition. What would you like to see your researchers invent? Make a wish list based upon your business focus, market, manufacturing capability and the other factors that make up a business plan. If you are a company that makes radios, you may have a wish list that includes a radio that will receive only music that the owner likes, it's programmable. (I would buy this.) Maybe the wish list would include a jogging radio with a rechargeable power supply that never needs a new battery, or a head set radio that actually works. (I would buy that also.) These are specific wishes and give the researchers a defined goal.

Next, you need to acquire the technical staff and technologies to work towards your goals. If you are the radio company just mentioned, you may need computer scientists to find ways to filter unwanted music and talk from the radio transmissions. You probably need an electrical/electronic engineer staff with expertise in electromagnetic wave transmission and filtering. You may need a battery engineer for the radio with the permanent power supply. You may need to hire a magician to make a headset radio that works. (Sorry, I go through at least two a year.)

> **RULE:** Research needs technical staff that is congruent with research objectives.

What we said about staff is also true about technologies. You need to become expert or buy the technologies that you need to meet your research objectives. The filtered radio project may need some kind of soundproof room to receive satellite signals or RF waves or some kind of RF wave generator. Whatever the project needs, you must get it.

> **RULE:** Some types of research need special equipment – get it.

Execution of a Research Strategy

Once you have a sound research strategy, how do you carry it out? First of all, you may have to teach your technical staff how to do research. In my many years in the business, I encountered many researchers who did not know how to do a research project. Most engineers and scientists who work in research organizations have graduate degrees that required a thesis. This is where researchers should learn to do a research project. There is a relatively simple format, but it must be followed:

1. Define the problem/objective
2. Establish the scope of the work
3. Study the work of others in the area of concern
4. Establish a project plan, timeline, staff, teams, budget, etc.
5. Perform laboratory studies
6. Review results
7. Reconcile results with work of others, explain unanticipated events
8. Draw conclusions
9. Make recommendations, implement work
10. Archive the results that may be usable to others

Many researchers repeat work that has already been done because they skip step three.

> **RULE:** Research requires a foundation of what is already known and what has been done by others – read the literature.

A project without a defined scope is on shaky ground. You cannot study the conductivity of all materials known to mankind if the goal is a plastic molding cavity with a faster cycle time. You will not have the time or money. You would limit the scope to a few classes of candidate materials, like tool steels or copper alloys.

> **RULE:** Researchers need to define the scope of
> their work and stick to it.

Many projects fail in the execution stage because they lack
basic organization. I will never forget one huge research
project that I worked on that involved many divisions and
hundreds of researchers. I got my part from somebody in
my division; he got his part from a larger team and so on up
the line. I tried for a year to find out who had ultimate
project responsibility and failed. After about two years into
the project, a symposium was called and we were asked to
give papers on our phase of the research. I thought, "Great!
I will finally find out who is in charge." Wrong! The
symposium was arranged by a peer of mine and the
symposium was chaired by a lower-level manager and I
still did not find out who was calling the project shots.
Needless-to-say, this 200-million dollar effort did not
produce a home run product. I think because of the fuzzy
organization.

> **RULE:** Let researchers know who heads the
> project, who is on the team, what is
> expected of each and when.

It is also necessary to keep everybody informed of what is
happening on projects that involve more than one person. I
like regular team meetings where everybody must tell what
they accomplished since the last meeting. On very large
teams, you can have sub-teams that report to team leaders
who meet to share information. Reports are essential;
written reports are needed, not data dumps on a computer
team suite. Many researchers do not like to write necessary
reports.

> **RULE:** Make formal reports mandatory on
> research projects – and use them.

The project leader should be the reviewer of reports from
sub-teams and teams and he or she needs to distill these
reports into a coherent summary for company executives.

Many researchers become so engrossed in their research
effort that they do not want to stop when their objective is
not met on schedule. Projects and research thrusts need a
quitting criterion and live by it. I had a coworker who was
working on a project that involved the use of lasers. He
ended up with an elegant lab with all kinds of lasers and
associated hardware. Lasers did not work for the intended
project. However, he tried to get funding to use his lasers
to do this and that. The company said, "No, we spent a lot
of money on this project. It did not work. We want to shut
down this effort and move on." The researcher persisted,
so his manager selected him for downsizing. When he was
informed of his termination, he locked himself in his lab
full of lasers and refused to leave. Security staff had to
forcibly remove him. He could not quit his research. He
had become addicted.

> **RULE:** Know when to quit a research project
> – and quit.

Team research, team engineering, and team manufacturing
were the bywords of the 1990's and beyond. There is a
prevailing belief in U.S. industry that a team rather than an
individual can better accomplish all manufacturing
functions. I agree that teams usually produce better
implementation of research than individuals, but teams
must be used properly. Teams can become like committees

and a camel is a horse designed by a committee. There are some things that are done better by individuals. For example, I have participated on committees charged with defining technical terms in my specialty. The published definitions produced by these committees often read like insurance policies and only confuse the poor novice trying to get a succinct definition of "galling." This happens when each person insists on his or her word or clause as part of the definition. I suspect that English dictionaries would only contain a few hundred words if committees or teams defined every term. It can sometimes be impossible to reach a consensus. Maybe that is why the entire U.S. economy depends on one person – the Chairman of the Federal Reserve, Alan Greenspan. Teams work best when there is a strong team leader to enforce tasks and to distill the work of the individual team members into a collective effort.

> **RULE:** Use teams to collect individual efforts and have team leaders who can meld them into project results.

> **RULE:** Do not over-team; they can become recreational – a diversion from work.

Summary

My company had a huge research staff that produced not very much in the line of saleable products or services. I think that this happened because some of the research fundamentals discussed in this chapter were ignored. Most notably, the company failed to define their business space and focus on it. They vacillated. One year, top executives would say we are an information company; next year they would say we intend to concentrate on providing services; the next year they said we are a software company. All that time, the only money coming in the door came from early consumer products. They could not decide on a business – after 80 years of making mostly consumer products.

They also screwed up staffing, organization, and implementation. I am of the opinion that they failed in all aspects of what is supposed to happen in research. Part of the problem was diversity. They put people who lacked research savvy in manager positions because of birth circumstance or other reason. We were not lead by the best of our numbers and it was not clear where we were going. My recommendation is do not do this. Know where you are going, get the right people to make it happen, then organize, track and work diligently. Then reward the workers and protect the intellectual property that they produce.

CHAPTER 14: Utilization of Engineering Staff

The Engineering Problem

When I retired, I worked in the company's worldwide engineering division, which was a very weak, very unsure parochial function. There was a prominent rumor on the factory floor that the division and the machine shop that services it would be sold. We all thought: To whom? Who would buy this pathetic shadow of an engineering function? They only had anticipated work for about 75% of the staff and they almost completely lost certain engineering technologies such as electrical engineering, chemical engineering, industrial engineering, materials engineering and software engineering. They retained reasonable mechanical and manufacturing engineering, but the division was an embarrassment to me. I remember what it used to be. What happened? That is what we will discuss in this chapter.

The fundamental problems were:

1. Managers did not know how to get work or what to do with engineers during a flat or downward business cycle.
2. Probably more than half of the staff did not want to work.

The latter problem may be unique to my old company, but probably not. If ten people sign up to do a volunteer function like clean and elderly person's unkempt yard, you will see a gaussian distribution of effort. Two people will knock themselves out, one person will work like a buzz saw, two will keep going and it goes down from there.

There will be one person who spends the day talking and drinking soda. This is diversity; people have different work ethics. Most companies have developed ways to minimize the low return for their money from slackers. My company seemed to promote slacking off. The more do-nothing teams you belonged to, the more you were esteemed by managers. If you skipped a "foo-foo" meeting to handle a plant shutdown, you were chastised. There was a culture in engineering to prioritize work on internal projects and avoid or do a lousy job on product or production problems. Needless-to-say, this lackadaisical culture did not set well with the business units, which had to pay for the engineering staff.

The other fundamental problem, managers who did not know the business, may not be common in U.S. industry, but any company that is affected can be in serious trouble. Technical abilities are no different than other abilities like playing the piano, golf, writing, speaking other languages, and giving speeches. If you do not do these things on a regular basis, you lose it. I played the clarinet for five years as a boy. I have not held one for over forty years. There is no way that I could play one now. I lost the skill. I lost my high school French for the same reason. I never practiced it.

Many engineering managers leave the business early in their careers and subsequently they do not know what technologies are important, what constitutes a qualified engineer, even what constitutes useful effort on the part of subordinates. They become "clueless" as we say here on the factory floor.

These clueless managers were not familiar enough with the business to know where to direct engineering efforts and they did not have contacts or prestige to get major projects funded by business units. Thus, the problem with many engineering functions in U.S. corporations is underutilization of their engineering staff. Companies are not getting the value from their engineering staff that they are paying for. The purpose of this chapter is to describe engineering problems at my company as an example of how not to run an engineering organization and to present suggestions on how to establish and maintain a vibrant engineering function. The chapter objective is fully utilized engineering staff and engineers who obtain career satisfaction from their efforts.

We will discuss the underutilization of engineering staff at my company, my proposal for re-organization from my exit essay, and then we will go into more detail of how to organize an engineering function for success and how to utilize an engineering staff to enhance company profits.

The Origin of Organizational Problems

The engineering department where I spent the last ten years or so of my career was in shambles. Regular downsizings were occurring while engineering needs increased asymptotically. Plant machinery was ancient and needed re-engineering. Product problems were rampant and needed engineered solutions. So why did they continually lay off engineers? I believe that is was because the customer's lost confidence in the engineering staff. The business units that held the purse strings did not see their problems solved in a timely basis. They were not aware of the technologies offered and possibly most important, there was a lack of rapport between engineering management and business unit management. They should have been on a first name basis with each other, yet many business unit managers never even heard the names of engineering managers. Because of diversity thrusts, these managers were hired from other companies or they were promoted to manager from some obscure low-level position (promoted because of race, etc.) Engineering managers were not the best or the brightest or even the most politically astute. We had an organization based upon diversity rather than talent and competency.

My exit essay presents a hint of the details of our problem organization:

Exit Essay: *Engineering in a Big Company – A View from the Factory Floor*

The company recruited me when I was still in graduate school. In those days, we did not have to look very far to an engineering job. We simply went to interviews at the student union and signed up for trips to visit various companies. One of the factors that made me hesitant to even take an interview trip to this company is that they were looking for a metallurgist to work in the ECM&U Organization. I had no idea what this organization did, and I had a hard time describing to my classmates what kind of an organization I was applying to. They were interviewing for jobs in research labs and product development departments. Everybody knows what goes on in these kinds of organizations, but nobody knew what an ECM&U organization did. The acronym stood for engineering, construction, maintenance and utilities. It was an organization of 2000 people and the acronym stood for the things that it did. The "engineering" meant designing the production machinery and buildings needed in manufacturing. The construction organization built the buildings; each major building contained a maintenance (field division) organization and the utilities division ran the power generating stations. Engineering, at that time, was broken into "areas." Area 1 did chemical piping;

Area 2 did feedstock delivery systems, and Area 3 was miscellaneous engineering. (I was hired in the Area 3 Metals Lab.) Area 4 did structural engineering; Area 5 did electrical design, Area 6 was HVAC and Area 7 was the prestige area that did the innovative machine design that allowed the company to be a world leader in their business.

These organizations functioned fine, but the company was continually growing and most of the 2000 ECM&U people designed and built the facilities to make more and more product. Later, the ECM&U Organization became "Facilities" and other plants also started to have "Facilities" organizations. It was a task recruiting technical talent into a "Facilities" organization because recruiters had to spend a lot of time convincing candidates that they would not be designing toilets. In the last 20 years or so, engineering within this company has been scattered to the wind. What is left of ECM&U is now WP&CD or some such acronym. The utilities division has been sold to a company whose only experience in the field was running a power generating station at a university – so I have been told. Maintenance is not done in many areas. In other areas, machine operators do it and the few maintenance organizations that remain repeatedly fix the same old dilapidated production machines. The Worldwide Engineering Division, of which I am a part, allegedly does production equipment design. However, the only worldwide aspect seems to me to be helping China. I know of no engineering connection with company plants in England, Australia, France, Brazil, India, Canada, Colorado, Massachusetts, or Texas. My observation is that the Worldwide Engineering Division simply subcontracts capital work to outside contract engineering firms. It is closer to a purchasing department. Engineering at this company is declining and many "engineering" departments are staffed mostly with people who do not have engineering *degrees. In fact, the company has not even been listed in the design journals that I read as a potential place for new engineers to work. It has a reputation in colleges as not being a suitable place for engineers to seek employment. In addition, the company has not replaced retired talent, and so there are no experienced engineers to mentor new engineers and to transfer technology.*

What should the company do about engineering? First of all, the company's engineering function needs to be simplified. The scores of engineering departments that exist need to be reduced to one. All engineering should be under the Chief Technical Officer and it should be made technology specific. There will be just two directors in the technical community, one for product research and development and one for engineering. The engineering director will have various departments under him or her that coincide with types of engineering:

- *Machine and manufacturing process design*
- *Process engineering*
- *Plant engineering*
- *Industrial engineering (includes all "soft" engineering functions such as environmental, fire protection, safety, statistics, etc.)*
- *Materials and manufacturing engineering*
- *Product Engineering (includes software design, network design, etc.)*
- *Sales Engineering (includes field engineers, competent, intelligent)*
- *Controls/software engineering*

The machine shops are now part of engineering, but they should be reduced to one shop at each plant to produce engineering prototypes and proprietary equipment. Outside shops should be contracted to do emergency repairs, spare parts, and other routine machining jobs. Capital equipment can be bid on by outside shops. Maintenance shops, if necessary, should be managed and staffed by operating plants. Construction projects should be bid by outside suppliers.

After this simplification, the director of engineering needs to re-staff to regain lost technology in each of the technology areas. This re-staffing needs to be coupled with an effective, continuing education and mentoring program. The "Technologist" classification needs to be eliminated and only people with appropriate degrees or a license should be called engineers. The use of technicians should be discouraged and when they are necessary, they should be called technical associates. There should be no salary cap on technical positions. Hierarchical titles such as senior engineer, engineering associate, etc. should be eliminated. These class differences are a big source of animosity in the company's technical community. Engineers can work in the fifty-six different business units, most engineering assignments will be rotating in nature and an engineer may work in ten or more business units and in the product research and development department in his or her career. All engineers will receive tours and training to let each know what kind of engineering is being done in research and various engineering groups in the corporation. There will be many forums for information sharing and technology transfer. There will be many collaborative teams.

Finally, engineering managers must be chosen based upon engineering competence rather than political

*considerations. One of the reasons for this company's
mess is "clueless leaders." The leader of the control and
software engineering department must have a work record
exhibiting excellence in this area. The leader of the
process-engineering department should be a chemical
engineer with a stellar record of accomplishments in design
of chemical plants. The company needs to get back into a
mindset that fosters technical excellence. Recruiting to
regain technical excellence cannot happen until there is an
organization that will be attractive to young professionals.
He or she will be able to visualize a career path that can let
the person move into different specialties and growth. The
company can go back to hiring the best from universities.
The company can start its comeback in business. My
opinion.*

My exit essay reflected my perception of organizational
chaos. The engineering staff was splintered into small
groups that worked for many unrelated organizations.
Some production departments had engineers on staff to take
care of production machine problems. They mostly worked
as maintenance staff. They kept machines running. Then
there were pockets of engineers who worked as product
engineers for business units. Most of these were product
trouble-shooters and not product engineers. They did not
develop new products and many had no engineering
credentials. Some production departments had
manufacturing engineers on staff who were supposed to
develop manufacturing processes, but spent much of their
time outsourcing machine shop work. The corporate
engineering staff had no links with these "pocket"
engineers and to add to the chaos, the company established
a consultant program that required redesign of all
manufacturing by the machine operators. There were no
engineers involved. In fact, the managers of this program

showed a complete contempt for engineers in their presentations to people on the factory floor.

I retired before I found out the extent of business damage inflicted by this latter program, but from the newspaper reports on business results, it appears that this program is greatly increasing the company's downward spiral.

How does this tail of woe at one company apply to U.S. industry? I went to a recent seminar sponsored by an industrial engineering organization and I walked away with the distinct impression that "Kaisen disease" as it is know on the factory floor has infected many U.S. corporations. In a nutshell, this program assumes that all industry involves making the same thing forever and business success is achieved by moving machines and people around to minimize motion and effort on the part of machine operators. This program appeared to be the industrial engineer's revenge for denigration received from classmates in engineering school. When I went to engineering school, you enrolled in one of four engineering programs; mechanical, chemical, electrical or materials. If you could not make it in one of these basic programs, you could fall back into industrial engineering. The math and science was less rigorous; industrial engineering courses were easier. Most industrial engineering graduates were made production supervisors or worked in methods departments where they dealt with plant layout and improvements in time to complete manufacturing operations. They did what industrial engineers were trained to do, but they usually never had a position of prestige in the corporation like the product engineers or machine design engineers. Now, through a program lathered in Japanese foo-foo, they get to run all of manufacturing and seemingly defy many of the engineering principals that gave them trouble in college.

It is not really that bad; industrial engineering has been ignored and it needs to be revisited in most companies, but it should be done in collaboration with other engineers. That is the fundamental organization problem. Different types of engineers and engineers in different organizations do not work with each other. There is very little collaboration of engineers in U.S. industry and engineering staffs need to be reorganized to make collaboration and synergy happen. They need official linkages. They need an overarching organization. They need to pull together to increase company profits and improve products.

> **RULE:** Do whatever is necessary to prevent chaos in any part of your organization.

How to Organize Engineering for Success

My exit essay presented some details on how a large company could organize its engineering function for success, but I left out many details for brevity. As mentioned previously, I wanted to spend my last year before retirement studying the company's technical staff and writing a white paper to recommend fixes for problems. The chief technical officer turned me down on my proposed study. So the organizational suggestions that follow lack the interviews and study of peer companies and I apologize for that.

I have a "pigeon-hole" mentality; I am a "neat-nick" and I absolutely disagree with chaos as a way to run any organization. Some people disagree with this philosophy. It's too bad. They are wrong. I can think of nothing that works without order and logic. At the time of this writing, the country of Afghanistan is trying to create enough order to keep forty million people from starving to death. Their current state of chaos is producing the starvation risk and the chaos is due to a lack of the order that comes from not having a government. So how does a corporation create order and collaboration for their technical staff? The most important first step is to establish a defined linkage between all technical staff. Make them members of the technical staff and all technical staff report to the chief technical officer.

In my company, this would be like a census. I suspect that they had absolutely no idea how many mechanical, chemical, electrical, etc. engineers they employed or how many technicians they employed. As I mentioned elsewhere, the human relations department can create titles that tell no one what an employee does. Once the various types of engineers and scientists are located, collaborative work, training and education programs can be established. These programs can cross division boundaries. For example, teams that write consensus standards for industry have representatives from many industries and controls are in place to give equal representation between users, manufacturers and general interest participants.

My company started to establish linkages between technical staff with common interests, for example, they established a forum for software engineers and another for mechanical engineers, but the collaboration consisted simply of running annual symposia. There were no actions directed at collaborative project work or career guidance. A visible career path is a very important part of any person's work life. This is especially true in engineering and research. Technical people like to see how they could move from one position to another and move through various divisions to some final goal. Politicians know that they can start their career as a helper in a political party; they can try to get elected to a party office; then run for city council, then mayor, then state assembly, then state senate, then governor, the U.S. representative, etc. They can visualize a career path because order exists in our government system. This kind of visualization is important and order needs to be created in a company's technical staff to allow employees to control their careers. They need to be in an organization that can be shown on an organizational chart. This was impossible in my company because every person in the company was operating as their own business. They empowered people to the point where they had 80,000 street vendors competing with each other to sell their balloons at a parade.

> **RULE:** Employees must be given a defined organization to work in.

> **RULE:** Technical staff must have linkages to foster their technology.

> **RULE:** Technical staff must have linkages to allow collaboration project work.

Of course every organization is different, but this book is intended to fix large manufacturing companies and typically, they will have the gamut of engineers and scientists on staff. My suggestion on how to establish linkages is to have the office of the chief technical officer operate like a contract research and engineering company. In the U.S., there are a number of these companies and they will have physicists, computer scientists, and materials scientists – the gamut. If a manufacturing company wants to eliminate a carcinogen in a product, they can get a quote on the necessary research. If the price is right, the research and engineering (R and E) company will assemble a team with the required technical specialties and give them a timeline to delivering the replacement. If another company wants a faster calendaring mill for paper, an engineering team can be assembled to do this job. If a company wants an invention, this can be an assigned project. Very few inventions come from divine inspiration. They come from a defined need. An invention team may be more diverse than the calendaring team, but it still needs a team assembled from available technical staff.

> **RULE:** Identify your technical staff and organize them to collaborate as needed on defined projects.

Essentially, I am recommending that manufacturing companies organize their technical staff into a coherent division/organization that can be contracted by business units for new products, manufacturing facilities, environmental problems, production problems, even business software. They are the company's technical resource; the technical staff has defined technologies; each technology is charged with being up-to-date and highly trained; various technologies will be called on to solve problems; technical staff can visualize which technology groups they may want to progress through in their career. Each technical professional will also have available funding for fundamental work, but progress and value will be continually monitored. The chief technical officer and all managers will be knowledgeable in all of the technologies that are available in the research and engineering organization and will have the education and work experience necessary to garner respect from employees in their charge. This is my model engineering organization – a contract research and engineering company with a modicum of fundamental "blue sky" capability. Will it work? Sure. Most technical universities work this way. Each technology maintains itself, mentors and teaches, but departments freely collaborate on major projects. What I am proposing is not weird. It is an orderly organization where needed technologies are nurtured.

How Do Engineering Departments Get Work?

Once a cogent engineering organization is established, the issue of project funding needs to be addressed. How do you run a research and engineering function? Where does the funding come from? How are projects initiated? Where does the work come from? The ideal situation would be that the priority projects for a research and engineering company come from the corporate product strategy. What improvements are needed in existing products? What new products does the company use for next year – three years hence – five years hence? Corporate executives must have the vision to direct the technical staff.

> **RULE:** Let corporate strategy drive research and engineering projects.

Top-down projects should even be discussed with the board of directors. However, you must make it clear to all what your business is. I witnessed the CEO's of my company vacillate to the point where nobody in the corporation seemed to know what the business was. Was it automobiles, home appliances, newspaper publishing? What happened to the business that we had for 100 years? Did it disappear? Not in my opinion, but our executive committee seemed to think so.

This rule means to not use meaningless or undefined words
in defining your business. For example, the government of
the state where I live just pledged fifty million dollars for
the establishment of an Infomatics research center. What is
Infomatics? Who knows? Employees and customers can
understand "plumbing," insulation," "ice cream," not
Infomatics, nanotribology, bioinformation and other
manufactured words. Use the language known to your
customer base.

Bottom-up initiation of projects should, firstly, come from
business unit managers and production managers. Where
are the product needs? Where are the production
problems? Where are the limiting factors in the
manufacturing process?

As I mentioned in my exit essay, years ago, managers ate
lunch together at many manufacturing plants. This practice
ensured that the managers, at least, knew each other. The
first five or ten years of my work life at my last employer,
my assignments came from the lunchroom. My boss would
say, "They are having a fatigue failure problem in the air
supply ducts in building 136. Go there and talk with Joe
Doe and resolve this problem." Sometimes it was a one-
hour job. Sometimes a year-long research effort. The
problem got solved in a timely manner without spending
fifty thousand dollars in meetings and approval paperwork.

Products were also identified in the lunchroom. Managers may have received increased complaints on a particular problem. He or she would then talk to the research director at the table by the window and an effort would be established to invent a new product or upgrade the existing product to eliminate the problem. The business unit manager should also be in daily contact with their sales staff to discern market trends and needs. These needs can be funneled through informal lunchroom contacts to appropriate research staff.

RULE: Have sales staff define market activities/needs regularly to the technical staff.

Manager intercourse does not have to be at the lunchroom, but someplace, somehow. It must occur. Many corporate managers do not know their peers much less collaborate with them. Managers must make the effort to know each other.

RULE: Make managers a team.

Another way to get technical needs to the technical staff is for all production managers to regularly review production results. They should track scrap, machine shutdowns, operation costs, cycle times, environmental problems, and people problems. These tracking results will identify production operations that need re-engineering or even product failings. This seems intuitive, but at my company, I never saw it done on a regular basis. Lots of departments would post process control charts, but when I scrutinized some of them, often they were just a smokescreen. They would plot weekly EPDD or some other acronym that served to camouflage operations. Then there were those managers who ignored tracking results. One division that I did work for used to measure machine shutdown times and completed units. For three years I watched, "waiting for product" to be the highest bar on the downtime tracking charts. Nothing was ever done to reduce the "waiting for product" problem.

> **RULE:** Act on identified product or
> production needs.

Finally, I recommend that work for the technical staff come from immediate supervisors and technical staff members themselves. I already advocated that even researchers should be given the opportunity to have one or two "blue sky" projects at all times, but when a member of the technical staff has a good idea, that may fit the company's business model, there must be a mechanism for this to happen. Engineers need to be able to make proposals for projects that they feel need to be done. Proposals can be submitted to a "funding committee" and projects that have the best business cases should be funded.

> **RULE:** Make project funding available through
> technical staff proposals.

The department manager that I had on my first engineering assignment used to spend a lot of time in his office reading magazines. We used to joke about him spending his day reading magazines. Years later I found myself doing the same thing only in my home office. I worked in a department that developed manufacturing processes for new products. My manager came up with ideas for new processes, largely from technical literature. Even today I still read at least ten technical journals as a regular basis and I somehow file information that may be helpful in future or current projects. My old manager was making sure that we were using the latest and most cost-effective manufacturing processes. We were cutting edge because he combed the literature for applicable technology.

> **RULE:** Engineering managers must supply project ideas and technical direction.

So there are my suggestions on how companies can get better utilization from their engineering staff. The difference between a market leader and its competition can be its technical staff and how effectively this staff is used. Many companies have competent engineers, but do not know how to apply them to the business. Do not let this happen – rule.

CHAPTER 15:   Work Life Quality

Attributes of a Good Job

What constitutes a good job? What does it take to create a company that people like to work for? I know that there are countless employee surveys that rank what people like and dislike in their work life, however, my observations over more than forty years on the factory floor produced this ranking:

1.   Job satisfaction
2.   Challenging job
3.   A trusted supervisor
4.   Trusted coworkers
5.   A reasonable physical environment
6.   Pay/promotions
7.   Reasonable benefits

Having all seven attributes comprises a good job. A single void in any of the first four attributes can make a job hell – my opinion. This chapter is a commentary on job attributes, things that affect the quality of work life. Its purpose is to present a view from the factory floor on how company managers should run the company so that most employees feel good about their jobs.

Why is it important to have happy employees? Miserable employees make faulty products, give poor service, have low productivity, steal from the company, and are unpleasant to be around. In other words, miserable workers are bad for business. Thus, the objective of this chapter is to increase business success through improved work life quality.

We will review my exit essay on work life quality and then explore how industrial companies should address our identified job attributes and make them positive for most employees.

What I Disliked At My Company

My exit essay will present my laundry list of gripes about my last employer. At this point, I would just like to reemphasize the importance of quality of work life. It has been my observation that when employees start to "bad mouth" their employer, the company's business starts to deteriorate. My mother worked for many years at a company that seemed bent on demeaning employees and continually taking away things that people needed to make their job easier. They were adversarial; the employees never talked well about the company and they went out of business after seventy years. My three sons all quit jobs because of quality of work life issues. They risked their careers quitting these jobs, but in each case, there were issues other than the "work" that made them quit -- a hostile work environment, a dishonest manager, an out-of-control management. My wife only had two jobs in her life and she quit one because she had a supervisor that thought that he was Napoleon. He made the twenty women in the department raise their hand when they wanted to go to the restroom. He sat at his desk all day reading Playboy magazines and often made off-color remarks to his all female staff. She quit because of poor quality of work life. It took some time, but this company recently went bankrupt after 80 years in business.

There are all kinds of psychological profiles for people in this world. There are also many interpretations of what is ethical. Some cultures even today accept taking the life of others. However, a business must set some standards of behavior or there will not be enough order to run the business. Similarly, there must be some checks on psychological profiles that lead to inter-employee friction. For example, pathological suck-ups create a hostile environment for coworkers. Dishonest managers do the same. Vulgar employees make other employees uneasy. Bullish employees do the same. Any employee who shows no consideration for others can cause an unhappy work environment. My company touted mutual respect, but allowed every employee to do whatever he or she wanted. They stated that they want the highest integrity from employees and regularly promoted dishonest people and unqualified people. They did not practice common sense in establishing a reasonable quality of work life.

> **RULE:** Make psychological profile and ethics a factor in hiring and promotion.

My exit essay discusses some of the personality and ethics factors that affected my work life.

Exit Essay: *Work Life Quality – A View from the Factory Floor*

What is it like here on the factory floor? Is the company a good place to work? Are we satisfied with the pay, benefits, and environment? Do we get satisfaction from our work? Are we proud to work for the company? Are we happy? What is the quality of work life? The company has many new top managers. They came in at a very high level and this precludes a first hand knowledge of what it is like to be an ordinary worker at this company. It is the purpose of this essay to provide one person's opinion (mine) on some of the factors that constitute work life at the company. Most employees are allotted some space - a place where we can hang our outerwear and keep some personal stuff. We

*are assigned to a particular building or plant; some are
nicer than others. We all interface with our coworkers in
aisles and in meetings. We are given rules and computer
systems that determine how we do things. We all want
promotions and raises; some organizations are better than
others in this regards. Finally, there is the company
culture that is mandated by top management. This essay
will present my opinion on the current status of some of the
major factors that contribute to the quality of work life at
the company. My list includes:*

1. *Physical environment*
2. *Company rules*
3. *Pay/promotions*
4. *Benefits*
5. *Culture*

*I will conclude each discussion with my suggestions on how
to make the quality of work life better for those who will
carry on after I leave.*

Physical environment *– My personal workspace has been
located within a sixty-foot diameter circle on the fifth floor
of the "engineering building" for all of my thirty-eight
years. I started with a three-foot by five-foot used steel
desk in an open area containing twenty more of these desks
for my coworkers. I had a phone and a bookcase for
reference books. It was a great physical environment for a
"green" engineer. I heard and saw how the experienced
engineers handled projects and they were always there to
answer questions and give direction. Our lab was only
about 50 feet from the desk area, so my world was centered
in a few building bays (the spacing between pillars). The
building itself was bustling with life. The first three floors
contained machine shops with every imaginable capability;
the other five floors contained the engineers that knew*

everything about the plant, designed the production equipment, built the buildings, and supplied the power. We were a contiguous team. We knew each other, what each department did, and where to go to get help to get projects done.

It was a wonderful, friendly, cooperative environment and the restrooms were spotless. And best of all, each had a shoeshine station for our use at no cost to us. In the 1980's our department expanded a bit and we engineers were given a reference table and the boss got an enclosed office. The company started cost savings programs and that is when the shoeshine stations were removed from the restrooms. This saved the cost of shoe polish and brushes. About ten years later we all got metal and glass partitions between desks. There was glass above desk height so we could still make eye contact and talk with our coworkers. In the early eighties, personal computers were introduced into our department. Only the boss' favorites had one the first year. Then it became a status symbol to have one. These gadgets were supposed to revolutionize engineering. You know the rest. Now there are computers on every desk and we live like moles in long rows of cubicles. Nobody sees anybody except at the coffee station, department copier or printer. People in my department left and I did not find our about their leaving for several weeks. Each person is a world unto him or herself. The not-so-ethical employees use their computer for personal business or entertainment. Everybody is encouraged to do everything on the computer and many employees cannot find a thing to do when their computers are down. I have seen engineering departments go home when their computers were down (and they did not work at CAD terminals). Most engineers use their computers for creating glorious spreadsheets, task shuffling, and accounting.

Besides the computers and the cubicles that comprise our present physical environment, the restrooms are filthy, with plumbing in bad repair and there is graffiti on the walls. Most cubicle clusters are dirty and disorganized. Overall, the plant where I work is a pigsty, not from excess equipment or materials, but from lack of consideration for others. I think that the company is a frightful work environment at present. Beside sloppy cubicles, dirty carpets, filthy bathrooms, employees do whatever they please without thinking about the impact on coworkers, their work output, or company results. I cannot think at my desk because the department secretary who is two cubicles away spends her day in idle chatter in a piercing voice loud enough to be heard throughout the eight-story building. A significant number of the people in the department have radios on their desks, each turned to a different station and playing loud enough to be heard in a four-cubicle radius. The office is a maddening cacophony of noise and the lab is worse. The contractors who do building maintenance use the passenger elevators to move heavy equipment even though the building has four huge freight elevators that work very nicely. In simple words, the physical environment in my part of the company is horrible. It is very very difficult to do work that requires concentration; there is no sharing of information; no collaboration, no helping others, no camaraderie. And worst of all, there is no one to complain to about other employee's lack of consideration. If you say something about another employee, you will be punished to such an extent that you will never say anything no matter what others do at work. People cannot say anything about their physical environment for the same reason. People just shrug their shoulders and hope to get through another day.

Company rules – I mentioned the "the company's values" in a previous essay, but these rules are probably the root *cause of the lack of consideration that makes the company's physical environment so horrible. We must respect the right of others to write on the bathroom walls. To complain about rap music coming from the next cubicle would probably be a violation of the integrity rule. Supervisors can use a "Taliban" type of interpretation and suppress all employee interactions and dialog or he or she could use the "values" as intended - a guide for reasonable employee behavior. The potential for "Taliban interpretation" is so high that I believe that these edicts often create an intolerable work place environment. I certainly would not recommend this company as a place to work to any person that I know or like.*

The safety neurosis that is practiced at the production plant is another work life aspect that is very distressing. In my department, we get daily safety e-mail messages forwarded from various places, and safety discussions dominate all department meetings. We must comply with ludicrous rules like recording the volume of acid used when we wet a cotton swab with several drops of acid to etch a small microscopic specimen. We even have to have safety data sheets on document correction whiteout. Yet there is no consideration given to us working in life-threatening conditions. It is okay to work for eight hours a day in methylene chloride fumes, or acetic acid fumes or airborne asbestos and silica particles. One time the company decided to replace the windows in our wing of the building. They used pneumatic tools to break the windows free from the bricks. For three months, we sat in a dust cloud. I had the dust from my desk analyzed and it contained 100 times the OSHA limit for silica. People became very sick, but our manager refused to do anything to have the demolition area sealed from our work area. However, do not get caught with a bottle of Windex or some other commercially available product without going through four hours of paperwork and record keeping. I suspect that many company managers are using safety rules as a smokescreen to cover up their lack of good ideas on how to improve the business. Safety minutia replaces management decisions on eliminating waste, improving machine operation time, improving profits and improving product quality. It is something that they can hype as important and gives them exposure to employees while hiding their inability to solve business problems. My disappointment with company managers is showing. Sorry. There are those of us who would like to see this company survive, but here on the factory floor where I sit, there is little that we can do to change things. In my opinion, only "anti-litigation" safety is practiced within the company. There is endless safety hype, but little practice of common-sense safety and the company does not seem to be concerned about the long-term health of its employees. (six people out of seventeen in my department developed the same type of cancer over the past ten-year period. One died).

The company's computer rules state that we are not supposed to use them to visit porn sites or any other non-business related site. These rules are probably the same as in all other large companies, but I wish that they enforced the rule to keep employees from using company computers for recreation and personal business. In my department, which is probably typical, I counted the number of people who spend at least several hours per day using their computers for non-company things. The number was nine out of seventeen people. I base this on my observations in walking around the department and how many people have non-company stuff on their screen when I drop into their cubicle with a question. Some people are even using the company's computers for day trading their retirement funds. In my opinion, not everybody needs a computer. If I were the CEO, I would require a business case for having a computer on one's desk. I would replace most individual computers with a carrousel of computers like they have in public libraries with the screens facing aisles for e-mail and other normal use. This would take care of a lot of the porn, and non-business use.

The other big failing of computers in this company is that we are not allowed to have the software that we need to do our jobs. In my organization, the computer operations have been turned over to some organization called TCP. I do not know if they are a company organization; I do know that the software that we must use is certainly not appropriate for engineering. There is a rule that we can only use TCP computers and that we must use the software that this organization, whoever they are, deems that we should have. We used to have all kinds of special software to run the testing machines in our lab. When we were forced into TCP, all of our computers were taken away and purged of the special software that we needed. It was replaced with the standard software that comes with home-use computers, and in my opinion it is essentially useless for scientific work. For example, since TCP, I have not been able to make a proper graph of experimental data. When they took away my computer system it also contained an expert system that cost the company $6000, a scientific data processing program that cost the company $2000, and probably the only copy of an expert system developed by the company at a cost of over $100,000. All of this was replaced with business and recreation software that is okay for e-mail, surfing the Net, simplistic business use and recreational use. I think that the company has created a debilitating, unnecessary cost by its proliferation of computers without business justification.

The last rule that I wish to discuss is the one covering document retention. We cannot keep any documents on the computer servers for longer than 45 days or the computer police will delete it. Also, we cannot keep printed documents more than one year without a hassle with the document police. These rules make us dispose of project data even before we complete the project. The organization that I am in actually sends out auditors to look in desk drawers and file cabinets. An illegal document will result in a summons. I suspect this Gestapo-like attitude on document retention started about 20 years ago. Documents were subpoenaed from various engineering departments (including my files) and the competitor's lawyers found some that showed reverse engineering data on their product. The company was sued by this competitor. The net result of these documents was a 970 million-dollar award to the competitor, and the shutdown of a business unit. This happened even though we made the product for the competitor for many years prior to the suit. We did not lose the lawsuit because of any incriminating documents. Every company who wants to stay in business will buy its competitor's product and pick it apart to see how it works and try to improve their system to be better than the competition. No, in my opinion we lost the lawsuit because my company had inept lawyers. Now we have a rule that forces a ludicrous file purge every year. Again the company punishes its employees and the business because of mistakes of previous administrations. The company needs to develop a common sense document retention system, one that does not hurt the business like the present one.

Pay/promotions – In simple terms, the company pays non-professionals and managers too much and professionals are paid about right – my opinion. We have technicians and machine operators with no formal education making in excess of $60,000, secretaries making over $40,000 and machinists making at least twice that of their local *counterparts in small shops. The key point is that the local labor markets would never pay these kinds of salaries for the skill levels that these people have (or do not have). My son, who works in a small machine shop, told me that when they recently expanded they tried to hire some machinists who were downsized or retired from this company. Over a six-month period they hired and fired about ten ex-company machinists; they just did not have the skills needed in a small competitive shop. Small shops cannot absorb mismachining losses like this company can. A similar situation exists with secretaries. Since we have computers on our desks we have been told that we must type all of our own documents, arrange all of our own meetings, handle our own expense accounts, use electronic passes for visiting suppliers, to submit expense accounts electronically, and to, essentially, do all clerical aspects of our jobs by ourselves. So what do secretaries do? In my department, she chats. At the next level up, secretaries seem to spend their time arranging the boss' calendar and so on up the line. Surely the company could have an outside service handle bosses' schedules at lower cost than the $40,000/year that a company secretary earns.*

On the top end of the too-much pay scale are company managers. All of us here on the factory floor have copies (from the "network") of company pay schedules at every level. As far as I can discern, the lowest paid company supervisor makes in excess of $100,000/year – way too much in my opinion. Then there are the vice presidents. In the last few years, almost weekly, we see in the news that the company has created another vice-presidency. By my count, it is about two per week. So there are about 100 new VP's each year and only a few retire per year, so my estimates are that the company now has about 15% of its employment as vice presidents (I may be off a bit, but you get the message). Since lowly supervisors make $100,000 per year, certainly vice presidents must make $200,000 per year. Surely, this is not good for net profits. I do not know why the company needs so many vice presidents, but I do know that we are not improving in the business world. So, I conclude that business success does not follow from VP creation.

Benefits – the Company used to have countless perks for all employees and benefits that were better than most other U.S. companies. After twenty years of benefit paring, I suspect that the company is now trailing most peers. Of course health care is the big cost. Each year we are told to pay more to get less. Coworkers with spouses working at other companies often opt for their spouse's benefits; they were better. (Note: here is a cost reduction suggestion -- one of my sons works at a small company that only covers health care of a spouse if the spouse does not work. The company may try this since many employees already use their spouse's benefits)

I am not in a position to compare the company's benefits with peer companies, but I can say which benefits I like and those that I do not need or want: First, those that I do not need:

1. Child care – my youngest child is 33 years old
2. Maternity – again, my youngest child is 33 years old
3. Disability – I am already disabled; besides I have a non-company policy
4. Nursing home care – I prefer to be a burden to my children
5. Low cost parking more than a mile from the building – the company loves to exercise employees, but I did not appreciate the thirty

minutes per day that I spent walking from the parking lot to the office.

6. *Bonus – it is not an incentive for improved performance it should be stopped*

These are the benefits that I like:

1. *Health care – what we have has been working fine and the cost to me is reasonable*
2. *Dental coverage – this is valuable to us; we use it*
3. *Flextime – I really appreciate that the company now allows me to start work within a ½ hour window rather than start at a buzzer.*
4. *Vacations – I have enough (six weeks after 35 years), but young people really need 3 weeks to start. Also, I resent having to use my vacation to go to technical conferences (I have had to do this for the past three years)*
5. *Lunch breaks – I really used to enjoy eating lunch after working for four hours, but for the past three years, my department has held its meetings and mandatory training sessions during our lunch break to reduce burden charges. We essentially lost the lunch break benefit.*

Overall, I think that the company's benefits used to be as good as other companies', but they have really slipped in recent years. Most employees want reasonable benefits, but they really would prefer a kinder and gentler company in lieu of some benefits. Many managers treat employees like dirt and there is no recourse.

Culture *– I have probably said enough about the effect of the company's diversity emphasis. Everybody is afraid to* *speak out about anything that they feel is not right. It is almost as if the company is trying to commit suicide. Most of us here on the floor just shake out heads and say: How can they do these things? How can they bring in diversity people to run a division when they have never even worked in a factory? How can they forbid straight talk? We cannot say that a machine or process is bad and needs improvement. This would be negative behavior and the value police would charge us? How can they keep ignoring the dirty production areas? How can they ignore shoddy workmanship? How can they keep people repressed in cubicles with no interface with other humans? It just does not make sense to have a culture that violates common sense and human nature. People do not want to be caged in cubicles. They would like to work in teams. They want to help the company. They want the company to succeed. So why are they doing these things to us?*

I think that the answer is that consultants have misguided company management. It seems as though company managers cannot think for themselves. They vacillate between conflicting programs from consultants. The company should try to regain the culture that we had thirty years ago. A change in the right direction would be to refocus on the business rather than somebody's social ministry. Next, the company should ask for behaviors that consider others. Then the company should try to rebuild its technical team, its infrastructure, its manufacturing equipment and start to value and listen to employees. This should be the company's cultural goal.

Summary *– The quality of work life at this company has changed significantly within my career. People used to love to work here. They would brag that they were second and third generation company employees. They used to praise the company wherever they went. The company had*

120,000 company ambassadors. Now we are 80,000 miserable employees, most of whom would like to leave, because it simply is no longer a nice place to work. However, if you are diversity, then it is the best place to work in the world. You will be given special treatment, preference for promotions, and you may not even have to do any work, simply be a figurehead. Of course, company managers will dismiss this essay and my others as the ranting of an angry, disgruntled, downsized employee. Well, I'm not angry anymore – just disappointed. I am disappointed that I could not turn the company around. I have spent the last three years trying to change things, to improve things, to get managers interested in new products. I failed and that makes me disappointed. I think that the company's scattered, uncollaborative technical staff is the root cause of our poor product showing.

I have run out of time to save the company. I have only fifty-eight hours of employment left. Shortly, I will be one of the many employees who have spent their lives here and when they leave it is as if they were never there. That is okay; I know that a corporation does not know the people that work for it and the corporation does not miss anybody when they leave. A corporation is not a person; you cannot hurt its feelings by never talking to it again. What will I do to keep trying to save the company? I guess that I will just continue to pray every day like I do now: Dear God, please save my company.

I ended my exit essay, essentially, by apologizing for not being able to save the company. I never got a reply from the CEO or executive vice-president. They obviously regarded this and my other essays not worthy of a reply. I suspect that they get dozens of letters each day from employees with gripes, so I am not surprised. Every employee probably has a shopping list of gripes. I think that mine were universal – they apply to all employees. The following are some rules to improve work life in a large manufacturing concern.

Physical Environment - Most employees do not care if they work in a fancy place, but they like it clean.

> **RULE:** Make housekeeping a priority in all
> company facilities.

All human beings are different and all deserve the right to their own space. Most human beings are civilized and socialized to the point where they respect the rights of others nearby and do not force their proclivities on them. I am writing this on a crowded airplane and the two hundred or so other humans on the plane are sitting in their seats and not shouting, whistling, singing or doing anything to annoy the 199 other humans in the ten-foot diameter, 140 foot long cylinder that we are enclosed in for an hour. One baby is an exception; she is crying, but she has not yet been exposed to rules for social behavior. Apparently, neither have my company's management. Allowing each employee to bring in a radio and leave it blasting all day in his or her work area is nothing but sheer lunacy. I realize that the company first allowed radio playing at work to ease the boredom for employees who had boring jobs. To this I answer, there is no way that a radio, TV, of any similar device with an audible output over the background sound can be operated in any company with more than one employee without annoying others. If I played a TV or radio in this plane, I would be annoying and infringing on the rights of the 199 other people on the plane. The same is true if I whistled or sang or shouted. No employee should be allowed to make noises that can distract others, and no employee has a right to use a radio at work since the company is paying these employees for their full attention, not two-thirds attention to the radio and one-third to work.

The cubicle syndrome is another aspect of my company's work environment that really bothered me. It is the antithesis of teamwork and collaboration. Nobody sees anybody that they supposedly work with. I realize that cubicles came about to minimize one worker distracting another worker, but distractions are certainly not reduced by a cloth covered wall. People in adjoining cubicles play radios tuned to different stations and talk loudly on phone calls. Present cubicles do not reduce distractions and they serve to isolate workers from there coworkers. Our research department often puts two researchers in one small office. This is even worse than a cubicle. Each person is a party to the other's phone calls and any noise-making activities. I have worked in all conditions from alone in an inspection room to one of forty people on an assembly line to a drawing board in a huge room full of others at drawing boards, to a desk in a big room full of other people at similar desks, to a shared office, to partial partitions between desks, to full partitions between desks to a cubicle. If I were CEO of my company, my first action would be to sell all cubicle partitions and direct all managers to rearrange their departments to let people see each other, but not hear each other's phone calls or discussions with customers, no radios, no noise above background noise, no unnecessary distractions.

> **RULE:** Do not put employees in cells (cubicles); use ingenuity to minimize noise and distractions.

There is not space to present details on how to design workspaces to eliminate the isolationism of cubicles, but I have visited many workplaces in European businesses and industry and they seemed to have learned how to make workspaces people and collaboration friendly. Nobody has a cubicle; managers may have an enclosed office, but with glass walls and door. There is no reasonable explanation of a cubicle; no company can survive for the long-term with them. In other words, I do not care for cubicles. I feel that they absolutely destroy teamwork, mentoring, camaraderie, and they promote people doing personal work on company time. They lead to sneaky people. They bring out the very worst in people. They are the concoction of the devil – my opinion.

In summary, the physical environment of my company used to be wonderful. Everything was spotless and orderly and after the consultants had their way with the executive committee, most plants were dirty; housekeeping was ignored; facilities were unmaintained; cubicles and general disregard for each other made up the typical work environment. Each person works as if a separate business is centered in his or her cubicle. They do not work with their coworkers or for company objectives. They work only for their personal survival.

Company Rules - All companies need to define acceptable behaviors. My company used to have unwritten rules that required professionals to wear shirts and ties, big bosses wore suits and everybody was friendly and considerate of their coworkers. The company diminished quality of work life by ignoring common sense safety in favor of phony safety initiatives that create a safety smokescreen that allows employees to die without lawsuits.

RULE: Be honest about safety.

The computer rules took away necessary software and replaced it with household trivia ware. Concurrent with diminishing the technical capability of computers, the company promoted the use of work computers for personal use by putting one on the desk of every salaried employee.

> **RULE:** Make sure people need computers
> before you give them one.

The company created their own six commandments and a company religion. This religion was interpreted by supervisors to produce whatever employee effect he or she desired. Anything that anybody did could be considered to be a violation of the six commandments. Sneezing during the supervisor's safety talk could result in terminal punishment.

> **RULE:** Keep socio-economic proclivities out
> of the business.

The document police were only a minor annoyance at my company. The sad part of their terror campaign was that just about all projects were repeated with each generation of employees because documents showing that the work was previously done were discarded.

> **RULE:** Archive documents that could be useful
> three and five years hence.

Pay/Promotions - Essentially, my company paid most employees far too much and made enough diversity managers to forever eliminate the possibility of having any cash on hand or company profits.

> **RULE:** Pay for results and make it
> commensurate with peer companies.

Benefits - My company had enough benefits to make all employees happy and pleased to work for the company. There was company paternalism and it was great. The benefits that we had when I retired were diminished to the point where they certainly were not sufficient to entice needed new talent.

> **RULE:** Give enough benefits to get and retain
> the best.

Company Culture - The company's culture was one of a family of loyal to death employees, each of who served as salespersons for quality products, who trusted their managers and executives and were happy at work. The culture when I retired was characterized by mutual distrust, discrimination in hiring and promotion, and general disregard for product quality and the business. What a shame!

> **RULE:** Strive for a company culture that includes
> all employees, the business, and ethics.

Unions - One subject that I did not mention in my exit essays or any other discussions is unions in U.S. industry. I said nothing in my exit essays because the company that I directed the essays to had no unions in the plant where I worked, but there were unions in some of their manufacturing locations, mostly outside of the U.S.A. My personal experiences with unions started with my mother's problems with her union and continued with my first few employers. My mother's union was one of the strongest in the U.S. and, essentially, she did not work for the company, but the union. If her supervisor gave her an assignment, she would have to ask the union committee person if she could do it. All problems were brought to the committee person and he or she would bring them to the attention of their immediate supervisor. There was a total dialog barrier between employees and the employer – the union committee person. My mother was forever having problems created by the union. I will never forget how she would have to take time off without pay to go to whistle-stop visits by Democratic Party politicians. Sometimes they would bring charter buses to the plant; shut down production and all union employees would be bussed to the political rally. If the rally was at a downtown hotel, my mother had to go to the rally on the city bus and pay for it herself. If the rally was outside of working hours, she was still required to go. The union committee people took attendance. After 32 years of hand sewing buttonholes on expensive suits, my mother's fingers were swollen and crippled by arthritis. She petitioned to the union to put her on easier-to-sew fabrics or another job. Instead, they gave her heavier military jackets. They made her retire. Her union pension was less than fifty dollars per month. Her union made slaves of the members.

> **RULE:** Do not depend on unions to stand up
> for their members.

My first working encounter with a union was at a factory that made steel desks. I was hired in as a paint inspector. It was one of the lowest paying jobs. The good paying jobs were all union jobs and the union people told me that I would have to work for several years as an inspector before they would consider me for union membership. The union employees seemed to be instructed to not fraternize with me. Inspectors were in some way linked to management. My next job was with the largest manufacturer in the U.S. (at that time). The union again was omnipotent. I was a coop engineering student and not eligible to join the union, but I would often be assigned to work as a helper to a union tradesperson, a millwright, a plumber, an electrician, a tool maker, etc. The union people that I worked for were always nice to me and showed me how to do their jobs. I never thought much about it, but I guess that I was doing their work for them. I still remember working for a toolmaker. He would set me up on a grinder to sharpen punch press die punches and go to the men's room to read a book. We were a great team until I screwed up and ran his beautiful grinding vice into the wheel. He watched me from then on. It seemed like I was one of them until the first strike that I encountered. I did not get paid unless I reported at the plant for work. When I tried to cross the picket line, the same employees who seemed to be my friends turned into angry mob members. They tried to stop my car; they bombarded me with insults. The union employees became adversaries of all other employees and the company. The strikes came on a regular basis and most times they were for more money for the same job. When I was given "white shirt" jobs, the union people shunned me. One time, I was the subject of a union grievance because I was seen walking down an aisle with a pair of pliers in my back pocket. The union committee person always seemed to be the department bully/loafer. The union contract allowed some fraction, maybe thirty percent, of the committee person's time to be away from his or her job to investigate union issues. Needless-to-say, they always found enough issues (like my pliers) to stay away from their job for the allotted time. A fundamental problem with unions appeared to me to be that the least, but loudest, of their lot was the leader.

> **RULE:** Encourage unions to pick their best, not loudest as their leaders.

My company kept unions out of most plants with their paternal culture and business success. People liked working there because of the pay, benefits, camaraderie, nepotism and the company's prestige. Unions happened when the company established a more aloof culture. I will never forget how union leaders handed me a flyer as I walked into the lunchroom at one of our plants in France. My French was not good enough to decipher all of the details, but the flyer headline read, "Un Grande Messe." No translation needed. They were after the plant management. I did not get involved in the dispute, but I observed that the workers had the "cushiest" work life that I ever observed. The cafeteria had gourmet food and wine at rock bottom prices and they had a two-hour paid lunch in which to partake.

> **RULE:** Unions do not help the business. Make avoidance a priority.

It is a shame that unions in the U.S. are in adversarial mode. They could be the employee advocates that many workers need. I suspect the problem is simply they lost their focus. Unions originated to mitigate unsafe working conditions and unfair wages. They became a business detriment by continually promoting undeserved pay and benefit increases. Their "my rice bowl" attitude on jobs also makes them a business detriment. Only a painter can climb a ladder; only a plumber can shut off a leaky faucet; only a millwright can move a printer stand. Teamwork and collaboration are impossible. In one of my company's plants, they had to make most employees salaried technicians so that they could be moved to different departments as product demands varied.

When I retired, I would have joined any available union in an instant because of the impossible management circumstances that existed in my plant. It was a horrific place to work. We workers on the factory floor needed an advocate to prevent worker abuses, discrimination, harassment and unfair practices. If a company does not provide advocacy, employees will turn to a union even though they may not be suitable advocates. What to do? Unions should refocus on their members' rights and become reasonable in pay and benefit demands. If most unskilled labor in an area makes $10.00 an hour, that should be the union demand (plus a little to cover union dues) – not $25.00 an hour as is currently the situation in the U.S.

If companies want one less administrative cost, they could eliminate unions as one. However, they must then learn how to listen to their employees. They need to provide a viable advocate function.

> **RULE:** Workers need advocacy.

Smoking - The final quality of life issue that I will discuss is smoking at my company. Up to about 1985, people smoked just about everyplace in U.S. industry where open flames would not cause a fire or explosion. One by one businesses and manufacturing companies curtailed smoking because of alleged second-hand smoke health risks to others. When I retired, the plant where I worked allowed smoking in "break areas" of every building. This was a considerate policy for smokers, but created a "less than happy" attitude on the part of non-smokers. Because smoking was only allowed in designated areas, workers had to leave their machines or desks and travel to and from the smoking area. In most buildings, this resulted in smokers only working 45 minutes out of each hour since they were allowed one break per hour. Smokers worked only 30 hours in a regular workweek. Non-smokers had to work 40.

> **RULE:** Develop an equitable smoking policy.

I could go on about many other things, but I think that I have adequately conveyed the things that concerned my coworkers and me on the factory floor. These are some of the things that contributed to, or diminished, the quality of our work life.

The Secret to a Quality Work Life

We conclude this chapter and this book with my proposal on how to improve work life quality and business success. I feel that they correlate and if I surveyed the literature, I am sure that I could find many concurring opinions. I purposely did not research business references for exit essays because I wanted to make this cut of this book a "spill my guts" expository. I want all business leaders to know how an ordinary worker, a worker who has never been a manager, feels about the management edicts that we have to live by in our work life. When an executive says that all employees should wear a white shirt and tie, how do we feel about that edict? When the executive committee declares that ninety percent of new hires must be designated minorities or special people, how do we feel about this? When the executive committee votes to give all employees stock options, how do we feel about this?

Secondly, I wanted this book to present my suggestions on how to improve the business. This sounds stupid since I previously stated that a corporation is a non-feeling entity, but I loved working at the companies that I worked for and loved the companies. They all had great products; they all had great potential. So why are three out of the five that I worked for in my career out of business? Ignoring the people on the factory floor was a contributing cause – I believe. How should businesses change to achieve success? I suggest adoption of the following as guiding principals:

1.   Good products
2.   Good marketing
3.   Mutual trust
4.   Mutual consideration
5.   Competency

How do these five guiding principals apply? These are my answers.

Good Products - This principal may seem intuitive, but I have observed that many businesses do not really care if they have products that differentiate them from the competition. In the restaurant business in the U.S., almost all restaurants have identical menus: Steak, pork chops, prime rib, chicken, filet of beef. This is the reason why my wife and I seldom dine out – same old. Most restaurants do not want to be best in their market.

> **RULE:** If you want to survive for the long-term, strive to be best.

If a company decides to be best, it has to do certain things to make this happen. If you want to be the best restaurant, you have to hire the best chefs and the best bartender and the best wait staff, and the best architect, and the best decorator, and the best landscaper, and the best maitre d'. You need a team of the best people. If you make durable goods, you need the best talent for product inventions, the best engineering staff to make the facilities, and manufacturing equipment, the best managers to run the factories. You need a team.

> **RULE:** Being best requires employing the best.

Good Marketing - It does not make any sense to have the best products if you do nothing to sell them. Going back to the restaurant analogy, you may have the best restaurant in town, but if the general public is not aware of this and where you are located, you will fail. You must market your good products at all times in all ways using every person that you employ.

> **RULE:** Marketing must be done by all employees at all times and it must be done in a way that differentiates you from the competition.

My wife monitors all TV, radio, magazines and outdoor advertising by my last employer. As I mentioned previously, she labeled it wholly inadequate and forgettable. They do not select the right venues; the advertisements that they produce for TV are shrugged off. They do not have the spark and humor needed to make the person on the street remember the ad or the product. "Where's the beef" commercials that everybody remembers do not come easy. So what? Find an advertising agency which can produce a "Where's the beef" or "I love New York" campaign. Demand results.

> **RULE:** Get the best advertising.

My company has poured many millions of dollars into the gas tank of a losing race car. In my opinion, this was a worthless venue. On the other hand, I witnessed them turn down opportunities to sponsor art and people events that would have produced immense exposure for little cost.

> **RULE:** Use common sense in selecting
> advertising venues.

Years ago, when people had time to cook, the companies that made cake mixes and baking supplies used to have a national cake-baking contest. They could get a million contestants offering a prize that cost less than $10,000. To me, this is the right venue and the right value. Sometimes, innovation is needed to get the best advertising. Something as simple as a minor lawsuit against a competitor can bring great press coverage. However, do these kinds of things cautiously. Recently, an airline let it out that they will charge fat people for two seats. It will probably take three years and many millions to recover from the negative customer reactions.

> **RULE:** Never produce an advertising campaign
> that can produce negative results.

The airline should have poled a segment of their customer base. They would have discovered the public empathy for being overweight.

Finally, a company can have good products and good marketing, but stretch the truth in advertising claims. Of course, to do so is a violation of business ethics and any violation has a way of backfiring. You cannot fool customers for very long and customers never forget. As I write this, there are scores of cell phone providers competing for my business. My wife will not allow me to have one because they have a monthly charge and she abhors monthly charges for anything. However, my sons and daughters-in-law have them and they tell me the only way to keep from getting socked with staggering long distance charges is to have a cell phone lawyer review all contracts before signing. Apparently, if you call from outside of designated areas, your ten cents per minute fee that you thought you bought can go to $4.00 per minute. It sounds to me like the entire industry is based upon customer deception. They are having a heyday now, but one competitor will emerge victorious by offering honesty and openness in advertising.

RULE: Dishonesty or deception in advertising will eventually lead to business failure; be open and honest in claims.

Mutual Trust - When I retired, one of the compelling reasons for my decision was the prevailing mutual distrust in my department, my division, and my plant. My coworkers distrusted each other because of impending layoffs. Each person connived to have the appearance of needed skills and subverted coworkers' attempts to prove that his or her work was important enough to preclude layoff. Survivalist mentality had kicked in and nobody trusted anybody. At the division level, directors were doing whatever for survival. At the organization level, big managers were competing with their peers for survival.

The weapons used by the managers were budget numbers. There was lots of creative accounting.

Before the integrity failure of the 1990's, in my company, for the most part, we trusted each other and management. Distrust was the product of many factors, but unqualified "diversity" managers were probably the root cause. They did not have the knowledge and skills to run the business and layoff fears spurred mutual mistrust at the factory floor level.

Any team, any organization that wants success must have mutual trust between members/coworkers. For the past twenty years or so, I had the help of a technician and machinist that I would trust my life to. I never had to worry about the quality of the work that we were doing or the honesty of our project results. They would tell me when we were on an errant path; they would fix designs that did not work as intended; they would freely offer suggestions to solve problems or improve an operation. There was complete trust in our tiny team. I have conducted numerous out-of-work projects with my family. The same mutual trust prevailed. I knew with 100% assurance that my sons would always contribute their all to make a project successful. I co-authored a book with one son, started a company with another and remodeled five rental properties with the whole family. Mutual trust made these projects successful.

> **RULE:** Business success requires mutual trust in all matters at all levels.

At the time of this writing, a number of billion dollar corporations are being flushed down the business toilet because of accounting irregularities – a euphemism for dishonest reporting of business results. There can never be mutual trust between these companies and stockholders, so their stocks are now worth only pennies.

Enron Corporation was dishonest with their employees and the net result was many employees lost their retirement savings. There will never again be mutual trust between current Enron executives and any remaining employees. There was not mutual trust between company executives and employees.

Finally, my coworkers who connived to underpin the careers of their coworkers lost. The entire department was eliminated because their mutual distrust manifested itself in phony answers to customers with technical problems (my prediction). Employee-to-employee trust did not exist.

Mutual trust between company and consumers is also imperative. I mentioned previously how my company stretched the truth in marketing a particular product. I complained vigorously to a vice president when I personally was dissatisfied with the product and they backed off on their deceptive marketing claim, but too late. There has been a study decline in market share for this product since this event.

> **RULE:** Customer trust is imperative and must not be risked.

Since about 1990, U.S. environmental agencies have been aggressively monitoring pollution events and regular contributions of manufacturing U.S. plants. It is highly desirable to establish mutual trust with these organizations. My last employer has had a number of multi-million dollar fines and government penalties can affect the business to a far greater extent than the fines. Customers may take their business elsewhere. They may not want to do business with a polluter.

I have witnessed blatant disregard for the environment in my career, I saw plating shops on the river with a chemical drain straight to the river, but in the old days, most manufacturers' facilities did not know the environmental consequences that they were bringing about. Up to about the 1980's, we did not have analytical equipment to detect trace chemicals in the air and ground water. When I retired, the company had analytical instruments that could check for 60 elements down to parts per million levels in a liquid sample in three minutes at a cost of only about $40.00. The environmental agencies also have this equipment. My company established a large expensive program to try and comply with all environmental laws, but the better way to approach environmental issues is with mutual trust. Become a partner with government and volunteer environmental groups. Trust them to identify harmful emissions and let them trust you to meet and exceed their standards.

> **RULE:** Make environmental concern part of every product and manufacturing operation.

Mutual Consideration - In simple terms, mutual consideration is the golden rule: "Do unto others as you would have them do unto you." Most civil laws are based upon this tenet. Murder is against the law because most of us would not like somebody murdering us. The same is true of stealing. Zoning laws enforce consideration between property owners. Traffic laws attempt to enforce consideration among drivers. Family members must practice consideration to make it possible for five people to live in a house with one bathroom. Mutual consideration is manifested between a company and its customers when they have a sales policy to do whatever is necessary to satisfy a customer. Companies are treating customers like they, as individuals, would like to be treated. Just this morning, I was cheated by a rental car company. I contracted for one day for a rate of $37.50. When I returned the car, the hand-held computer spit out a receipt for $248.00. After a twenty-minute haggle, I got the daily rate reduced to $58.00. Needless-to-say, I was dissatisfied and I will never do business with this company again. That is the way we customers are – show lack of consideration and we part paths.

Lack of mutual consideration within a company manifests itself by rudeness in the workplace, playing a radio with others in hearing range, talking loud on the phone when others are near, not observing company rules on using passenger elevators for freight, ignoring phone messages, not answering e-mail – many, many ways. Each time that a person lacks consideration with a coworker or manager, it drives apart teamwork and collaboration, and that can affect business success.

> **RULE:** Practice consideration in all people and business matters.

Competency - The dictionary definition of competency is having the knowledge and ability to satisfactorily perform a given task or in a given job. In industry, if you are hired as an engineer, you should have a degree from an accredited engineering school and be able to demonstrate that you can successfully complete engineering projects. If you are hired as a secretary, competency would be typing 150 words per minute, phone skills and proficiency in office computer software including budgeting. If you are hired as the vice-president in charge of a large manufacturing facility, you should know how to control costs, how to budget, how to solve people problems, how to garner support from subordinates and you must have demonstrated these skills for a significant amount of time in a peer industry. You must know all aspects of business and be a consummate "people-person." My company's diminishing business results were mostly due to incompetency in management produced by diversity initiatives – my opinion. They hired and promoted designated minorities because of the birth circumstance rather than competency.

> **RULE:** Demonstrated competency is a must for hiring and promotion.

Besides hiring for competency, a thoughtful company will encourage continued competency. You can hire the best finite element-modeling analyst, but if he or she does not keep abreast of changes in this rapidly changing field, he or she would soon be incompetent. Continued competency can be encouraged by simply making it a factor in performance evaluation. Ask every employee what have you done in the last six months to improve your competency, your skills, your job knowledge, and your value to the company? Make it a significant part of an employee's evaluation. If the employee's job is to assemble springs on a shaft, ask him or her what they did to learn other related jobs, or to increase their speed, or what suggestions they made to simplify their job or save money? Maybe just staying healthy can be a performance factor. Everyone must have a continuous improvement/growth plan.

> **RULE:** Employees must be encouraged to learn
> their job and continuously improve.

My company, after many false starts, made every employee chart a career path and training program each year. This plan was reviewed at evaluations. It did not work well in my department because the supervisor did not know the field and could not advise employees on needed training. Some employees did nothing but recreational things and told the supervisor it was necessary training. Thus, management competency is imperative. Clueless managers very quickly become the pawns of unscrupulous and unethical employees.

> **RULE:** Require managers to know the
> business that they manage.

Competency completes my five secrets to a happy work life. I am certain that a happy work life on the part of employees correlates with business success. When employees loved my company and bragged that they worked there, the company was successful and the products were of the highest quality. Now that employees cannot wait to retire and "bad-mouth" the company, business results are in the toilet. Employees are happy when they can trust their coworkers and management, when the products are good and well marketed, when employees and managers show consideration for each other, and when competency becomes contagious. Of course, ethics must prevail in all personnel and business matters. There can be no business success without ethics.

Summary

I pledged to write this book about fifteen years ago, when the corporate "shenanigans" began. The executives of my company were taken under the spell of consultants who never worked in a factory. They sold them one bizarre program after another. Sometimes I would muse: Is this really happening? Do they really think that grown men and women will perform better if we are given a star to stick on our forehead (really, we had this)? Do they really think that making me hug the big sweaty welder sitting next to me will endear her to me and vise-versa? Do they really think that hiring a transsexual person as director of product engineering will improve our products? Do they really think that blaring rap music played over the public address systems of offices will improve our work life quality?

I vowed that I would answer these questions in a book that I would offer to the world. My book would let corporate managers see how an ordinary worker on the factory floor feels about their shenanigans. My perspective is there for consideration. The goal of spilling my guts to management is to incite rejuvenation in American industry. I want corporations to stop the "shenanigans," to adopt common sense, to focus on the business and restore American industry to the prominence it had in the "BC" era (BC = before consultants). I want ethics to rule all management decisions, all interpersonal relations, all environmental matters, all financial matters, and all customer matters. I want an end to the type of customer deception that prevails in the service industry, the insurance industry, the investment industry and many others. I want corporations to be proactive in protecting the environment, not strategizing on how to avoid EPA rules. I want an end to discriminatory practices that are disguised as diversity. I want **ALL** people to have a chance to work. I want corporations to develop useful new products, not annually repackage same old. I want American manufacturers to make products that are better than the competition. I want companies to phase out human relations departments and replace them with service providers specializing in benefits and staffing. I want all companies to have advocacy programs to arbitrate and resolve problems without strikes and management retribution. I want lots of changes. I want to see more American business success.

Why only American business success? I have not worked outside of the U S.; so, I do not know if the rest of the world has been subjected to the "shenanigans." If business consultants have visited them, then I guess that they also need this book.

I purposely sanitized my writing and did not mention the company or its products and I am writing with a non-de plume so people cannot look up my address and ask my neighbors where I worked. I worked someplace in the U.S.A. and I think that what I wrote in this book applies to many, many U.S. companies. If nothing else, people who read this book will get a detailed perspective of the mental condition of a once-healthy male after spending forty-three years breathing the air on factory floors. Thanks for reading this book and remember: ethics is imperative.